JUNIOR CERTIFIC

LESS STRESS
MORE
SUCCESS

Religious Education
Revision

Niall Boyle

Gill & Macmillan

Gill & Macmillan
Hume Avenue
Park West
Dublin 12
with associated companies throughout the world
www.gillmacmillan.ie

© Niall Boyle 2011

978 07171 4711 3

Design by Liz White Designs
Illustrations by Keith Barrett
Print origination by Carole Lynch

The paper used in this book is made from the wood pulp of managed forests.
For every tree felled, at least one tree is planted, thereby renewing natural resources.

For permission to reproduce photographs, the author and publisher gratefully
acknowledge the following:

© Alamy: 15C, 15B, 45T, 55, 56T, 56B, 59, 75, 95, 100R, 100L, 101T, 101B, 103, 106,
109T, 109B, 110T, 114, 138B, 145; © Bridgeman: 31, 33, 53T, 134; © Corbis: 13, 15T,
35, 39, 41, 64, 69, 92, 117B, 138T; © Getty Images: 2, 8, 16, 19T, 20, 53B, 56R, 57, 62,
65L, 72, 88, 89, 113, 117T, 126, 136; © Imagefile: 45B, 46, 116; © John Stuart
Clark/Brick: 86T, 86CL, 86BR; © Press Association: 82; © Photocall Ireland!: 11, 68;
© Rex Features: 19B; © TopFoto: 76; Courtesy of Samaritans: 5; Courtesy of The
Simon Community: 4; Courtesy of St Vincent de Paul: 9.

CONTENTS

Introduction

The aims of Junior Cycle Religious Education are:

- to provide students with a framework for encountering and engaging with the variety of religious traditions in Ireland and elsewhere,
- to promote an understanding and appreciation of why people believe, as well as tolerance and respect for the values and beliefs of all,
- to prepare students for the responsibilities of citizenship.

Source: Department of Education

Syllabus overview

Students can choose to take Junior Certificate Religious Education at either Higher level or Ordinary level.

The syllabus is divided into two parts.

Part 1

Students may study *any two* of the following:

- **Section A** Communities of Faith
- **Section B** Foundations of Religion: Christianity
- **Section C** Foundations of Religion: Major World Religions (choose one from Judaism, Buddhism and Islam).

Part 2

Students must study *all three* of the following:

- **Section D** The Question of Faith
- **Section E** The Celebration of Faith
- **Section F** The Moral Challenge.

These sections can be studied in any order.

Note: Material that is to be studied only by those taking Higher level is indicated in the text.

Revision

Revision is the final stage of preparation for your exam. It is very important to make the most of it. Whether you are taking the exam at Higher or Ordinary level, you should do the following:

- Plan your revision schedule in plenty of time before the examination.
- When drawing up your list of topics for revision, make sure it includes all those areas required for the level you intend to take.
- Set out a daily timetable of work and stick to it.
- Give equal attention to all sections of the syllabus, including any areas you find difficult or uninteresting.
- Keep a positive frame of mind. A sustained effort will achieve worthwhile results.
- Try to minimise any distractions.
- Study for periods of 30–40 minutes, and take short breaks of no longer than 5–10 minutes between study periods.
- Familiarise yourself with the exam paper: layout; time allowed for each section; and marks awarded for each section.

Assessment

This has two elements: a **pre-submitted journal work booklet**; and a final **two-hour written exam**.

In the exam, the **Higher level** paper has **five sections** and the Ordinary level paper has **four sections**.

There are 500 marks available in total, for both Higher *and* Ordinary level.

- The journal work is worth 20 per cent of the total = 100 marks.
- The exam paper is worth 80 per cent of the total = 400 marks.

Journal work

- Both Higher level and Ordinary level students must complete the journal work component.
- You must choose **one topic** from a list of approved titles and submit your finished work in a special booklet provided by the State Examinations Commission.
- Titles for journal work are the same for both Ordinary level and Higher level.
- While you may work in groups or undertake a visit or investigation as a class, **you must submit an individual journal for assessment**.
- Use the cues/prompts down the side of the booklet as they will help you to **stay focused on your title.**
- You may draw diagrams/illustrations in the journal booklet, but **do not** attach any material to the booklet.
- Your finished booklet should be submitted for external examination along with your exam paper.

Journal booklet checklist

Section 1 – Introduction

○ Have you indicated whether you did this journal work on your own or as part of a group/whole class?

○ Have you identified the title you chose from the prescribed list?

○ Have you given a relevant personal title to your journal work?

○ Have you stated the reason why you chose this title?

○ Have you described what you hoped to find out by doing journal work on your chosen title?

Section 2 – Getting started

○ Have you described the way you planned to work on your chosen title?

○ Have you identified the skills you used?

Section 3 – Work

○ Have you described the work you did (either as an individual or as part of a group)?

○ Have you stated the reason why you chose this way of doing journal work?

○ Have you described your reaction to the work you engaged in on your chosen title?

Section 4 – Discoveries

○ Have you identified what you learned from doing journal work on your chosen title?

○ Have you described the effect doing this journal work had on you?

○ Have you identified two skills used in doing journal work on this title and described how you used them?

○ Have you identified two links between your journal work and other aspects of the Religious Education syllabus?

Section 5 – Looking back

○ Have you reflected on and evaluated how you approached doing journal work on your chosen title?

○ Have you indicated what went well?

○ Have you identified how you would do your journal work differently if you were starting again?

Note: you can find further information on the journal booklet at the State Examinations Commission website, www.examinations.ie.

Concerning dates

Traditionally the following abbreviations have been used for dates: BC = Before Christ; and AD = Anno Domini (Latin for 'In the year of Our Lord').

However, in this book the abbreviations BCE (= Before the Common Era) will be used instead of BC, and CE (= Common Era) will be used instead of AD.

How the exam is marked

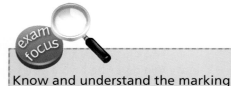

- The Religious Education exam paper may be taken at either Higher level or Ordinary level.
- In each case, **400** marks are awarded in total for the written paper.
- At Higher level, the paper has **five** sections; at Ordinary level, the paper has **four** sections.
- Each section contains different kinds of questions.
- A specific amount of time is allotted to answering each section. Keep within the time indicated.

> Know and understand the marking scheme, in particular the marks and percentages given to each question on the paper.

For example:

Higher Level Marking Scheme Total marks = 400					
Section	Question Type	Marks Available	Time (minutes)	Number of Questions	Number to Answer
1	One-line/ tick box	50	15	20	Any 10
2	Visual-based	30	15	4	Any 3
3	Article-based	50	15	4	All
4	Detailed analysis	200	55	6	Any 4
5	Short essay	70	20	6	Any 1

Ordinary Level Marking Scheme Total marks = 400					
Section	Question Type	Marks Available	Time (minutes)	Number of Questions	Number to Answer
1	One-line/ tick box	80	20	20	Any 10
2	Visual-based	60	20	4	Any 3
3	Article-based	60	20	5	All
4	Detailed analysis	200	60	6	Any 5

SECTION A

Communities of Faith

1 Community

aims
- To understand the meaning of community.
- To identify examples of community.
- To know the characteristics of community.
- To understand the strengths and weaknesses of community.

key point

A community exists wherever two or more people have something in common, e.g. living or working together, sharing similar interests, or holding broadly similar views about life.

Examples of community

Local
- family/friends
- school
- drama group
- musical society
- residents' association
- sports club

National
- political party
- charitable organisation, e.g. Society of St Vincent de Paul
- trade union

International
- Friends of the Earth
- Red Cross
- Trócaire
- United Nations Organisation

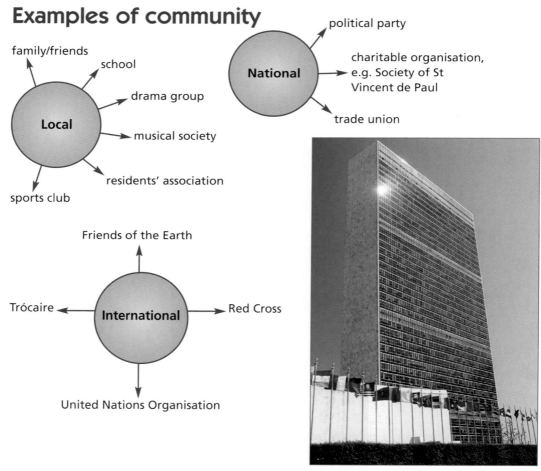

The United Nations headquarters in New York City

Characteristics of community

- **Co-operation** – working together to achieve a common goal.
- **Sharing** – dividing resources fairly and using them for the benefit of all.
- **Communication** – listening to one another and exchanging experiences, feelings, hopes and ideas.
- **Role** – the specific part played by a member of a community, e.g. leader, counsellor, organiser, fund-raiser.

Strengths of community

Communities help us to fulfil our different needs. For example:

- **physical needs:** food, water, clothing and shelter
- **emotional needs:** to be loved and respected for oneself
- **security needs:** a stable, orderly and safe place in which to live/learn/work.

Weaknesses of community

Community breakdown can occur:

- when people fail to share, co-operate and communicate
- when the needs of some people (e.g. the homeless) are ignored and they are left isolated
- when some people (e.g. refugees) are deliberately made to feel unwelcome.

2 Communities at Work

- To know about the work of two national charitable organisations.
- To understand the vision that inspired this work.

key point

- Vision – the important idea that motivates people to work together to achieve a goal.
- Leadership – the exercise of power by a person in authority who guides people to achieve a goal.
- Service – doing something for the good of others.
- Commitment – being dedicated to completing a task or fulfilling a role.

Charitable organisations

The Simon Community

Communities of Ireland

Background and vision

- Founded in England by Anton Wallich-Clifford in 1963.
- He was inspired by the work of Catholic social reformers, e.g. Dorothy Day (USA) and Mario Borrelli (Italy).
- He wanted to create houses of hospitality in which both the homeless and the housed would live in community.

Service offered

- First Irish centre opened in Dublin in 1969. Others were later set up in Cork, Dundalk and Galway. Together these form the national federation called the Simon Community of Ireland.
- These centres assist thousands of homeless people each year. They offer friendship and practical assistance, e.g. clothing, soup runs, safe places to sleep.
- Homelessness is a growing problem in Ireland. People can help the homeless by fund-raising and campaigning for more affordable housing.

Samaritans

SAMARITANS

Background and vision

- Founded in 1953 by Rev. Chad Varah, Anglican Rector of St Stephen's Church, London.
- He was particularly concerned with helping to reduce the number of suicides.

Service offered

- Samaritans volunteers support distressed people who call a helpline.
- The volunteer listens to whatever the caller has to say, which can help the caller feel less isolated, see a problem in a new light and find a way to cope with it.
- This service is available 24 hours a day, every day of the year.
- There are more than 18,000 volunteers in over 200 branches of Samaritans in the UK and Ireland.

Rules followed by all Samaritans volunteers

- The confidentiality of a caller's identity is guaranteed.
- The caller will never be contacted by Samaritans unless he/she wants it.
- There is no 'message' except that there is someone ready to treat the caller with respect and listen to whatever he/she has to say.
- Volunteers are known to callers only by their first name, e.g. 'Michael 6' or 'Joanna 2'.

3 > Communities of Faith

- To understand the meaning of a community of faith.
- To know the founder(s) of each of the world's major religions.
- To identify common characteristics of communities of faith.
- To understand the meaning of vocation.
- To know about the work of one religious organisation at national level.

- Faith – belief in, love of, and trust in God.
- Community of faith – exists wherever people share the same religious beliefs and practices.
- Revelation – the way God communicates with human beings and allows them to know things they could not know by their own efforts.
- Founder – a person whose teaching and example leads to the establishment of a religion.

Types of religious belief

- Monotheism: the belief that there is only one god.
- Polytheism: the belief that there are many gods.
- Henotheism: when a person believes in one god but does not deny the existence of other gods.

The communities of faith

There are five major world religions.

Religion	Founder(s)	Date
Hinduism	Unknown rishis (wise men)	c. 2000 BCE
Judaism	Abraham	c. 1800 BCE
Buddhism	Siddhartha Gautama	c. 586 BCE
Christianity	Jesus Christ	c. 7–4 BCE
Islam	Muhammad	622 CE

Common characteristics

1. Inspiring vision – the powerful idea that first led people to accept and spread religious beliefs.
2. Creed – a clear statement of the beliefs shared by all members of a community of faith. *Example:* the Shahadah in Islam – 'There is no God but Allah, and Muhammad is his prophet.'
3. Moral code – a set of guidelines that help people to decide whether an action is right or wrong. *Example:* the Ten Commandments for Christians.
4. Ritual – a religious ceremony in which God is worshipped and believers celebrate or mark important moments in life. *Example:* a ritual of initiation, e.g. baptism for Christians.
5. Place of worship – a place or building where believers gather to worship God. *Example:* a synagogue for Jews.
6. Calendar – marks the passage of time and indicates the holy days of a particular religion. *Example*: Easter for Christians.
7. Sacred text – the holy book or scriptures containing the important stories and key teachings of a religion.

Religion	Sacred Text
Hinduism	The Vedas (also the Bhagavad Gita and the Upanishads)
Judaism	The Tenakh (or Hebrew scriptures)
Buddhism	The Pali Canon (contains the Tripitaka)
Christianity	The Bible (containing the Old and New Testaments)
Islam	The Qur'an (pronounced 'Koran')

Sacred text as a document of faith

A sacred text is considered a 'document of faith' for all/some of these reasons:

- It was inspired by either God or the founder of a religion.
- It tells the founding story of a religion.
- It outlines the basic beliefs of a religion.
- It offers guidance on how to live a good, moral life.

Vocation

The meaning of vocation

All the major world religions teach that their members should show their commitment to their religious beliefs by the way they live their

key point

- Vocation – the sense a person has of being called to serve God in a particular way.
- Religious commitment – making a firm decision to live out one's religious beliefs in daily life.

lives. This involves fulfilling one's vocation through ministry, i.e. by helping others. People may minister to others through their commitment to family life, work or voluntary organisations.

Some people believe that their vocation is to commit themselves full-time to do certain work as members of a religious community. For

A Buddhist monk

example, in Buddhism and in some Christian traditions (e.g. Catholic, Orthodox and Anglican), a person may enter religious life as a monk (if male) or a nun (if female).

In the Christian tradition, a monk or a nun may belong to a specific religious order. Orders can be one of two kinds.

- Apostolic communities work in the community, e.g. caring for the poor, the sick and the homeless.
- Contemplative communities live enclosed lives. Their members rarely, if ever, leave their monastery or convent and they devote all their time to prayer, study and manual labour.

After completing their training, all monks/nuns must take the same basic vows (solemn promises):

- poverty: not to be tied down by worldly possessions but to share their goods
- chastity: to refrain from sexual relationships and devote all their energies to prayer, study and good works
- obedience: to be completely dedicated to God and work for the good of the community.

All monks/nuns live according to a rule (a detailed code of conduct). The most famous of these is the Rule of St Benedict (6th century CE).

The work of a religious organisation: The Society of St Vincent de Paul (SVP)

Society of St Vincent de Paul

Background and vision

- Founded in Paris by Frédéric Ozanam in 1833.
- Ozanam was a university professor. He was appalled by the poverty he witnessed in the slums of Paris. He believed one could only call oneself a Christian if one followed the example set by Jesus and helped those in need.
- The organisation Ozanam founded took its name from St Vincent de Paul (17th century), a Catholic priest who dedicated his life to serving the poor and disadvantaged.

Service

- SVP has branches in 112 countries.
- Its members seek to build a more just society, where wealth is distributed fairly.
- It offers friendship and a range of services to people trapped in poverty and despair. Its aim is to help those people to become self-sufficient.
- Each volunteer takes on a specific role in the organisation, e.g. home visits, prison visits, counselling, budgeting advice, providing hostels for the homeless, running shops offering affordable clothes and furniture.

4 Relationships Between Communities of Faith

- To understand the meaning of inter-faith dialogue.
- To identify examples of inter-faith dialogue.
- To distinguish between the four Christian traditions.
- To understand the meaning of ecumenism.
- To identify examples of ecumenism.

- Inter-faith dialogue – the members of the different world religions talking with and listening to one another.
- Pluralism – the belief that all religions have an equal right to exist.
- Tolerance – acceptance of and respect for the different religious beliefs and practices of others.

Inter-faith dialogue

Inter-faith dialogue is rooted in the ideas of pluralism and tolerance. The purposes of inter-faith dialogue are:

- to achieve mutual understanding, i.e. to gain a clear idea of what each other believes
- to combat prejudice and prevent conflict between people of different religions
- to work together on matters of common interest, e.g. combating injustice and poverty.

None of the major world religions believes that one religion is just as good as another. The followers of each religion believe that their religion offers the best and most complete set of answers to life's great questions. Inter-faith dialogue is rooted in the idea that all religions can learn from one another and work together to make the world a better place.

Examples of inter-faith dialogue

World Peace Day

- Held regularly since 1986 at Assisi in Italy.
- Pope meets representatives of other Christian and non-Christian faiths for a day of prayer for peace.
- At the 2002 meeting all agreed on the Decalogue of Assisi for Peace, which states that religious differences must never again be a motive for violence.

National Day of Commemoration

- Held annually at the Royal Hospital, Kilmainham, Dublin, on the Sunday nearest July 11.
- Commemorates all Irish men and women who lost their lives in past wars or on service with the United Nations.
- The day begins with a multi-faith service comprising prayers, hymns and readings offered by senior representatives of the different communities of faith in Ireland.
- This event communicates the idea that all faiths, both Christian and non-Christian, enjoy equal status in Irish society.

The National Day of Commemoration

Christianity: Four traditions

All Christians claim to be followers of Jesus Christ. However, over the centuries Christians have divided into four different

- Identity – <u>characteristics</u> that distinguish one person or group from another and so allow us to recognise them.
- Tradition/Church – an organised community of Christians which has developed its own distinctive set of beliefs and practices.
- Denomination – a particular branch of a religious tradition.

traditions: Catholic, Orthodox, Anglican and Protestant.

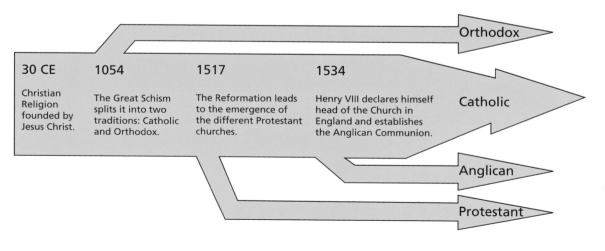

30 CE

Christian Religion founded by Jesus Christ.

1054

The Great Schism splits it into two traditions: Catholic and Orthodox.

1517

The Reformation leads to the emergence of the different Protestant churches.

1534

Henry VIII declares himself head of the Church in England and establishes the Anglican Communion.

Orthodox

Catholic

Anglican

Protestant

Each Christian tradition can be divided into different denominations (branches).

Christianity: Areas of disagreement

There are three main areas that divide Christians:

1. The meaning and number of the sacraments.
2. Whether or not the Pope is the head of the whole Christian community.
3. Whether women should be ordained or not.

The Denominations		
Catholic →	Roman rite	
	Uniate rite	
Orthodox →	Greek	
	Russian	
Anglican →	Church of Ireland	
	Church of England	
Protestant →	Methodist	
	Presbyterian	

Sectarianism

Sectarianism has caused great suffering throughout history. Over the centuries, there have been many vicious sectarian conflicts that have torn religious communities apart. *Examples:* between Catholics and Protestants in Europe; between Sunni and Shia Muslims in the Middle East.

Sectarianism – a narrow-minded, hostile and intolerant attitude towards people who do not share one's beliefs.

Ecumenism

The purpose of the ecumenical movement is not to try to make all Christians the same. Its aims are:

1. to promote mutual respect and understanding between the different Christian traditions

Ecumenism – the attempt to heal the deep divisions between Christians of different traditions that have arisen over the centuries.

2. to encourage Christians to co-operate in fulfilling the mission Christ gave his followers to spread his message across the whole world.

This can be achieved through:

- praying together, where possible
- engaging in open dialogue on the issues that divide Christians
- co-operating on issues of moral/social importance.

Examples of ecumenism

Taizé: An ecumenical community

- Taizé is in southern France.
- The aims of this community are to work for Christian unity and to express the Christian message in modern terms.
- Taizé was founded in 1944 by a Protestant named Roger Schutz (died 2005).
- The community is made up of people from over 25 nations and all four Christian traditions.
- All permanent members take three vows:
  1. to live a celibate life
  2. to share all their goods
  3. to accept the authority of the prior (community leader).
- Ecumenical prayer services are conducted in several languages three times a day: morning, noon and evening.
- Young people flock to Taizé from all over the world. There are now other groups modelling themselves on Taizé dotted around the world.

Brother Roger Shutz, founder of the Taizé Community

The World Council of Churches: Ecumenism worldwide

- The World Council of Churches (WCC) held its first meeting in Amsterdam in 1948.
- Its headquarters are in Geneva, Switzerland.
- Its aims are to promote Christian unity and to work for peace and justice.
- The establishment of the WCC was an initiative by different Protestant churches. They believed that the divisions within Christianity were damaging its mission by giving non-Christians a very poor impression of Christianity and so obstructing the spread of the Christian message.
- The WCC holds a general assembly every seven to eight years. Delegates discuss issues of common concern, such as human rights, poverty, climate change and refugees.
- A practical expression of the WCC's religious moral vision was the setting up of the overseas aid agency Christian Aid, which helps people in the developing world.
- At first the Catholic Church and the Orthodox Churches were not represented at the WCC, but the Orthodox Churches have been represented since 1961 and the Catholic Church has sent observers since 1968.

5 Organisation and Leadership of Communities of Faith

 Note: Part 5 is for Higher level students only.

- To understand the meaning of leadership.
- To appreciate the role of a religious leader.
- To identify the types of religious ministry.
- To distinguish between the types of organisation in Christianity.
- To examine leadership and authority in two Christian churches.

The role of the religious leader

Depending on the particular community of faith, religious leaders can perform some or all of the following roles:

- **Leadership** – directing, guiding or influencing others towards the achievement of particular goal(s).
- **Authority** – the power and responsibility a person in a leadership role has to make decisions affecting others.

- Interpreting the stories and teachings contained in sacred texts, and explaining their relevance to believers' lives today.
- Leading people in worship.
- Preserving the authentic doctrine (teachings) of the religion and guarding against heresy (false teachings).
- Encouraging the handing on of traditions (accepted teachings and practices) from one generation to the next.
- Setting a good example for others to follow.
- Encouraging people to convert (change) and join their particular community of faith.

Examples of ministry

The rabbi in Judaism

- The title rabbi means 'my master' or 'my teacher'.
- A rabbi is someone employed by a Jewish community to have authority over the running of a synagogue.

Ministry – the specific role a person plays in a community of faith.

- Rabbis are usually male, but some Jewish communities employ a female rabbi.
- A rabbi is not a priest. He/she is a lay person who has studied for several years to assume a leadership role in the Jewish community.
- A rabbi conducts weddings and funeral services, visits the sick and may act as a chaplain to schools, hospitals or prisons.
- He or she also gives the sermon at the synagogue services held each Sabbath (Friday evening and Saturday morning).

The priest in the Catholic Church

- The word priest comes from the Greek word *presbyteros*, meaning 'elder'.
- A priest is a man who has been ordained, which means that he has received the sacrament of holy orders from a bishop.
- A priest must remain celibate, i.e. be unmarried and not have sexual relationships.
- A priest is expected to: offer spiritual leadership to his parish (local Christian community); administer the sacraments (e.g. celebrate Mass, hear confessions and baptise new members); and explain the Church's teaching through sermons and/or discussion.
- A priest may serve as a chaplain to schools, hospitals or the armed forces, or as an educator in schools and colleges.

The imam in Islam (Sunni tradition)

- The title imam comes from the Arabic word meaning 'leader'.
- An imam is the learned spiritual leader of a mosque, which is the religious, social and educational centre of a local Islamic community.
- An imam is a layman, not a priest. He is selected for the position of imam because of his deep knowledge of the Qur'an and commitment to the Islamic way of life.
- He gives the sermon and leads the prayers in the mosque. He also teaches the Qur'an to Muslim children.
- An imam is often called on to give advice on a wide range of issues affecting the daily life of Muslims, such as selecting a name for a newborn child.

HL Types of organisation in Christianity

The different Christian traditions are organised in one of two ways:

1. Episcopal: where there are bishops in authority over a Christian community (e.g. the Catholic, Orthodox and Anglican traditions).
2. Non-episcopal: where there are no bishops in authority over a Christian community (e.g. Protestant denominations such as Baptists and Presbyterians).

Examples of organisation in Christianity

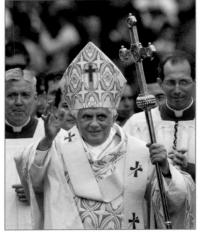

Pope Benedict XVI

The Catholic Church

- The largest Christian denomination: worldwide membership of over 1.3 billion people.
- Catholics belong to either the clergy – ordained members (i.e. bishops and priests); or the laity – non-ordained members.
- The task of guiding the beliefs and moral actions of Catholics is the responsibility of the Magisterium: the teaching authority of the Catholic Church.
- The Magisterium consists of the Pope and the college of bishops under his leadership. They are believed to be the direct successors of the original 12 apostles.
- The Pope is acknowledged by Catholics as the visible head of the Church and is given the title Vicar of Christ (meaning Christ's representative on earth).
- Each pope is elected within a few weeks of his predecessor's death by a conclave (closed meeting) of cardinals (i.e. clergy who are entitled to cast a vote).
- There is usually at least one cardinal in each country that has a substantial Catholic population.
- Bishops are appointed by the Pope to lead the people of an area called a diocese.
- Each diocese consists of a number of parishes, each led by a priest.
- The laity assist the priest as ministers of the eucharist, ministers of the Word, sacristans, catechists and choir members.

The Church of Ireland

- The Church of Ireland is a self-governing Christian denomination with about 400,000 members on the island of Ireland.
- The Church of Ireland is a member of the 70 million-strong international Anglican fellowship of independent churches.

- It is in communion with the Anglican Church in England (the Church of England) but is completely autonomous (separate). It is not under the authority of the Archbishop of Canterbury.
- The Anglican Archbishop of Armagh is the leader of the Church of Ireland.
- Church of Ireland bishops attend the Lambeth Conference, held every ten years, to discuss important moral and religious issues with the leaders of other Anglican churches.
- Any decisions reached at the Lambeth Conference must then be debated and accepted by the governing bodies of the individual Anglican churches before they take effect.
- The Church of Ireland has a democratic system of government.
- The General Synod is the chief decision-making body of the Church of Ireland. It meets every year and consists of two parts, the House of Bishops (12 members) and the House of Representatives (216 clergy and 432 laity).
- Each diocese holds its own local synod once a year to elect the diocese's representatives to the General Synod.
- At parish level, decisions are made by select vestries – groups of people who are elected each year by their local congregation.
- The Church of Ireland ordains both men and women to the ministry and they may marry if they wish.

Religious communities in Ireland today

Name of Church/Religious Group	Title of Leader
Catholic Church	Primate of All Ireland (Catholic)
Church of Ireland (Anglican)	Primate of All Ireland (Anglican)
Presbyterian Church	Moderator
Methodist Church	President
Jewish Community	Chief Rabbi
Islamic Community	No national leader: each mosque has its own imam
Baptist Church	President
Salvation Army	General
Society of Friends (Quakers)	None

HL Past Exam Questions

Section 1 (All questions carry 5 marks each)

1. Communication is a characteristic of communities. Name another characteristic of communities.

   Sharing

2. Read the lists of religious leaders and world religions given below. One leader has been matched to the religion with which he is associated as an example for you. Make **one** other match.

Leaders	Religions
Abraham	Buddhism
Jesus	Christianity
Siddhartha Gautama	Hinduism
Muhammad	Islam
Brahmins	Judaism

   Example:

Jesus	Christianity

   Answer:

Siddartha Gautama	Buddhism

3. In religious traditions, the term 'creed' means:

   _____

4. Read the lists of sacred texts and world religions given below. One sacred text has been matched to the religion with which it is associated as an example for you. Make **one** other match.

Sacred Texts	Religions
Vedas	Buddhism
Hebrew Scriptures	Christianity
Qur'an	Hinduism
Tripitaka	Islam
Gospel	Judaism

   Example:

Gospel	Christianity

   Answer:

Qur'an	Islam

5. Polytheism is the belief in:

   Many gods

6. Which of the following world religions is an example of polytheism?

   Christianity ⬜   Hinduism ✓   Islam ⬜

7. In religious traditions, the term 'vocation' means:

   a feeling of being called by God to serve others

8. Tolerance between communities of faith can be seen when people are willing to respect different religious beliefs and opinions.

   True ✓   False ⬜

HL

9. In religious traditions, sectarianism means:

Hatred of other people because they belong to a different religion

10. 'Moderator' is the title of a leader associated with the Presbyterian church.

True ◯   False ☑

Section 2

1. This is a photograph of a religious sister serving the needs of others. (2007)

    A. Pick **one** thing from the photograph which suggests that this religious sister is serving the needs of others.

    _____

    _____

    (2 marks)

    B. Name **one** example of a community.

    School

    (2 marks)

    C. Suggest **two** reasons why people need to live in a community.

    i. _____

    _____

    ii. _____

    _____

    (6 marks)

2. This is a photograph of people sharing in a community of faith. (2009)

    A. Pick **one** thing from this photograph which shows sharing among the people in this community of faith.

    _____

    _____

    _____

    _____

    (2 marks)

HL

B. Give **one** other example of a way in which sharing can be seen in a community of faith.

_____

_____

(2 marks)

C. State **two** reasons why sharing is important for members of a community of faith.

i. _____

ii. _____

(6 marks)

3. This is a photograph of a World Peace Assembly in Assisi. (2004)

A. Pick **one** thing from the photograph which suggests that this is an example of inter-faith dialogue.

_____

_____

(2 marks)

B. What is inter-faith dialogue?

_____

_____

(2 marks)

C. Give **two** other examples of inter-faith dialogue.

i. _____

ii. _____

(6 marks)

Section 3

(This section is worth 50 marks.)

Read the following article and answer *all* the questions below. (2004)

The Taizé Community

The Taizé community was founded by Brother Roger. As a young man he had been seriously ill. During his illness he decided to set up a community where the Gospel would be lived out in simplicity and kindness. In 1940 Brother Roger left his native Switzerland and went to live in eastern France, settling in a small village called Taizé. When the Second World War started Brother Roger made Taizé a place of welcome for groups as varied as refugees fleeing the war, French war orphans, and German prisoners of war. Gradually other young men joined Brother Roger in Taizé. On Easter Day 1949, the first brothers took vows to live as a religious community.

Today there is a community of about one hundred brothers. The brothers do not accept gifts or donations for themselves. They give anything they receive to the poor. Taizé continues to be a place of welcome for families uprooted from their lands – Vietnamese, Rwandans, Bosnians, etc. Taizé brothers have also gone to live with people who are suffering because of poverty or conflict in Asia, Africa and South America.

Over the years, the number of visitors to Taizé has continued to grow. Every week from early spring to late autumn, tens of thousands of people, mainly between the ages of 17 and 30, gather in Taizé. Visitors come from different countries all over the world. Some are from different church backgrounds and some from none at all.

While people come to Taizé for different reasons, all are searching for meaning or a deeper relationship with God. While many are active in churches at home, others have difficulty in finding a church where they feel welcomed and listened to. Some come for a chance to meet other Christians their own age or for an experience of community rooted in the Gospel.

It can be a life-transforming experience to spend a week listening to people talking about faith and the search for meaning in life. An important part of the Taizé experience is making links between Christians of different denominations by praying and working together. The Taizé community has welcomed church leaders like the Pope, the Archbishop of Canterbury, Orthodox metropolitans, Lutheran bishops, and countless religious ministers from all over the world.

Life at Taizé is centred on prayer, work and hospitality. Three times a day the bells ring out and everyone, brothers and visitors alike, stops what they are doing and heads towards the Church of Reconciliation. In the church visitors join the community in worship. People join in a form of meditation in which praying in song and silence plays a large part. The community likes everyone to take part in the singing even though visitors speak many different languages. To overcome this difficulty the brothers composed simple tunes with few words that are easily learned.

Each day groups of people meet with the brothers to reflect on and discuss the Bible. Every afternoon at 5 p.m. people stop for tea and those who come from

HL

different continents talk about their countries and their hopes. Visitors also help with practical tasks like cooking and cleaning and everyone shares in serving the needs of the whole community. The Taizé community encourages people to take home what they have discovered and put it into practice in their lives. It also organises regional meetings where people from different countries come together and plan how they will contribute to the life of their Church, and work for justice, peace and reconciliation at home.

Source: Ateliers et Presses de Taizé and Gill & Macmillan

1. Some people say that Taizé helped them in their search for meaning in life. From your reading of this article explain **one** way in which the experience of Taizé can help people in their search for meaning. (12 marks)

2. Religious belief can find expression in a variety of ways. Pick **two** of the following and explain how the experience of Taizé can help people express their faith in this way.
   ◆ Prayer   ◆ Way of life   ◆ Worship   (12 marks)

3. The Taizé brothers have faced and still face many challenges. From your reading of this article identify **one** challenge, past or present, and describe the Taizé community's response to it. (14 marks)

4. How does this article show what is meant by any two of the following:
   ◆ Reconciliation   ◆ Religious commitment   ◆ Vocation   (12 marks)

Section 4

1. (2009)

A.

(a) Explain **two** reasons why belonging to a community of faith could be important for a person. (12 marks)

(b) Communication ⬭   Co-operation ⬭

Tick (✔) **one** of the above and explain why it is important for a community of faith. (15 marks)

B.

(a) In religious traditions the term 'sectarianism' means:

_____ (5 marks)

(b) Describe **one** example of the way in which a community of faith is working to overcome sectarianism. (18 marks)

2. (2008)

A.

(a) In religious traditions, what does the term 'vocation' mean?   (5 marks)

(b) Outline **two** ways in which people live out their vocation in a community of faith you have studied.   (14 marks)

B.

(a) Describe **two** things that inspire the religious commitment of members in a community of faith you have studied.   (16 marks)

(b) Community breakdown ⬭   Religious conflict ⬭

Tick (✔) **one** of the above and outline the way in which it is dealt with by a community of faith you have studied.   (15 marks)

3. (2007)

A.

Giving direction is one way a person can lead a community. Outline what is involved in **two** other ways of leading a community that could be used by a leader.   (20 marks)

B.

Explain how the way in which a community is led can have an effect on its members.   (20 marks)

C.

Being a leader is one role a person can have within a community. Describe **another** role a person can have within a community.   (10 marks)

4. (2004)

A.

Tick (✔)**one** of the following world religions you have studied:

Buddhism ⬭   Christianity ⬭   Hinduism ⬭   Islam ⬭   Judaism ⬭

Describe the work being done today locally or nationally by a church, religious organisation or order associated with this world religion.   (14 marks)

B.

Outline **one** way in which the work described above helps people to live as a community.   (16 marks)

C.

Outline **one** way in which the work described above reflects the founding story of the world religion you have ticked.   (20 marks)

Section 5

(Each question is worth 70 marks.)

1. Discuss the effect that an inspiring vision can have on a community of faith. (2004)

2. Outline how a community of faith you have studied shows a sense of:

    i.   Commitment

    ii.   Vision.   (2007)

3. Profile **one** community of faith in Ireland today that you have studied using the following headings:

    i.   Inspiring Vision.

    ii.   Ministry.   (2009)

4. Outline **two** styles of leadership found in a community of faith.   (2005)

5. Outline the way in which leadership within a community of faith involves:

    (a) authority

    (b) service.   (2008)

6. You have been asked to write an article about the organisation and leadership of **one** community of faith you have studied. In your article you should refer to the importance of **two** of the following:

    ◆ Co-operation   ◆ Sharing   ◆ Communication.   (2003)

7. (a) Outline one example of inter-faith dialogue that you have studied.

    (b) Discuss the reasons why people take part in inter-faith dialogue.   (2006)

SECTION B

Foundations of Religion: Christianity

1 The Context

aims
- To understand the geography of Palestine.
- To know how Palestine was governed.
- To be aware of the different reactions among the Jews to Roman rule.

key point
- Holy Land – the name given to the area of the Middle East where the story of Jesus took place, i.e. modern Israel and the Palestinian Territories.
- Roman Empire – the vast territory, stretching from northern England to the Persian Gulf, ruled from Rome.

Palestine

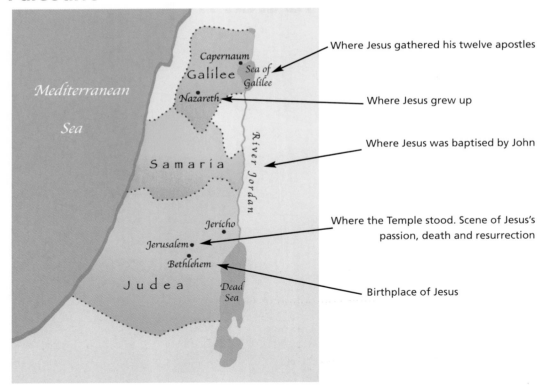

Palestine in the first century CE

Two thousand years ago, the Holy Land was known as Palestine. It was a province of the Roman Empire.

Size

Length (from north to south): about 240 km (150 miles).

Width (from east to west): 50–80 km (30–50 miles).

Political regions

As you can see from the map, the principal political regions of Palestine were:

- Galilee in the north
- Samaria in the centre
- Judea in the south.

Challenges

Life was difficult because:

- though the area around the Sea of Galilee was green and fertile, much of the landscape was sand and rock and therefore unsuitable for farming
- there were periodic droughts
- the sirocco (hot east winds) could strip away dry topsoil
- plagues of locusts could devour crops.

How Palestine was governed

- Herod the Great ruled over Palestine on behalf of the Roman emperor until his death in 4 BCE.
- Then the emperor appointed a procurator (governor) to administer Samaria and Judaea. One of Herod's sons was made tetrarch (commander) of Galilee.
- The Roman procurator of Samaria and Judaea between 26 CE and 36 CE was Pontius Pilate.
- His job was to maintain order among 750,000 people, keep the trade routes open and make sure taxes were paid promptly and in full.
- However, Pilate had only a garrison of 3,000 soldiers at his disposal to do all this. So he needed the help of the Sanhedrin.

The Sanhedrin

- The Sanhedrin was the ruling council of the Jewish religion.
- It was based in the Temple compound in Jerusalem.
- It acted as a court, with powers to punish any Jews who broke their religion's laws, and had its own armed force, the Temple Guard, to enforce its decisions. However, it could not impose the death penalty.
- It was composed of 70 Jewish elders who elected a High Priest to oversee its activities; however, the Romans could remove the High Priest if he displeased them.
- Its membership was divided into two rival groups – the Sadducees and the Pharisees.

Tax collectors

- As subjects of the Roman emperor, the Jews had to pay heavy taxes.
- Tax collectors were Jews willing to collect these taxes.
- Tax collectors were despised by most Jews and treated as social outcasts.
- They were not allowed to hold any religious office or to give evidence in court because they were considered to be dishonest and treacherous.
- Jesus shocked many people by inviting a tax collector named Matthew to become an apostle.

Jewish expectations about the Messiah

- The Jews had messianic expectations, i.e. they believed that God would send a messiah (from the Hebrew word *moshiach*, meaning 'anointed one').
- Most Jews believed that the Messiah would:
    1. free them from Roman occupation
    2. establish an independent Jewish kingdom
    3. bring peace and prosperity.

Jewish reactions to Roman Rule

By the first century CE, four groups had emerged among the Jews. Each reacted differently to Roman rule.

1. Sadducees

- A small powerful group composed of the High Priest, Temple priests and wealthy aristocrats.
- They dominated the Sanhedrin.
- They accepted Roman rule and used their influence to help the procurator fulfil his mission.
- They rejected belief in life after death.
- They did not expect a messiah to liberate them.

2. Pharisees

- A large powerful group composed of lay religious teachers (rabbis) who controlled the local synagogues.
- Unlike the Sadducees, they rejected Roman rule but did not actively oppose it.
- They devoted all their energies to living rigidly according to the laws of their religion.
- They believed in life after death.
- They expected a messiah to emerge from their ranks to free them from Roman rule and establish an independent Jewish kingdom.

3. Essenes

- A community of monks who devoted their lives to prayer, fasting and study.
- They rejected Roman rule but did not actively oppose it. Instead, they separated themselves from the rest of society and established communities in remote desert areas.
- They believed that they alone had the correct interpretation of the Tenakh (Hebrew scriptures).
- They may have been the authors of the Dead Sea Scrolls.
- They expected two messiahs: a priest who would restore the Temple; and a warrior who would free them from foreign control.

4. Zealots

- Members of a movement of deeply religious Jews who sought to overthrow Roman rule by violent rebellion.
- They hated the Sadducees for co-operating with the Romans and sometimes carried out assassinations of Sadducees.
- They expected the Messiah to be a warrior king who would end foreign domination and establish an independent Jewish kingdom.

2 Evidence about Jesus

- To know about the Christian and non-Christian sources for the life of Jesus.
- To appreciate that the four gospels are four versions of the one gospel.
- To understand the stages in the development of the gospels.

- Witness – to give evidence about what one has seen and heard.
- Gospel – means 'good news'; tells the story of Jesus of Nazareth.

Non-Christian sources

Document	Author	Date
Antiquities of the Jews	Josephus	c. 90 CE
Jewish Talmud	Various rabbis	Second century CE
Letter to the Emperor Trajan	Pliny	c. 110 CE
The Annals	Tacitus	c. 115 CE

Information Provided	Source
Jesus was a wise teacher and a miracle worker who appealed to both Jews and Gentiles	Josephus
He was condemned to death by Pontius Pilate	Josephus
This happened on the eve of the Jewish feast of Passover	Talmud
The execution happened during the reign of the Emperor Tiberius	Tacitus
Jesus's followers believed that he had risen from the dead	Josephus
His followers worshipped him as God	Pliny

Christian sources

The New Testament consists of 27 books that were written in the latter half of the first century CE. They are classified as follows:

Title	Number	Purpose/Content
Gospels	4	Record the life and teachings of Jesus
Acts of the Apostles	1	Describes the expansion of Christianity
Epistles	21	Offer advice to the early Christian communities and clarify key teachings
Book of Revelations	1	Predicts the triumph of God and the final judgment of human beings at the end of time

- The earliest known *complete manuscript* of the New Testament is the Codex Sinaiticus (4th century CE).
- The earliest known *fragment* of the New Testament is the Rylands Papyrus, a fragment of John's Gospel, dating from 134 CE.

The Rylands Papyrus

The Gospels

- The word *gospel* means 'good news'.
- There are four gospels: Mark, Matthew, Luke and John.
- The authors of the gospels are called evangelists, meaning proclaimers of the good news.
- The first gospel to be written was Mark, c. 64 CE. The last was John, c. 90 CE.

The focus of the Gospels

- The gospels do not offer a biography of Jesus in the modern sense of the word. For example, they do not include a physical description of him.
- The evangelists were more concerned with explaining the meaning and importance of Jesus's life. They wanted to persuade people that Jesus was the promised messiah.

Four versions of one Gospel

- There are four gospels.
- Each gospel includes details that the others do not. For example, Matthew and Luke begin their accounts with the story of Jesus's birth, while Mark and John begin with the adult Jesus.
- They differ in certain details, but each evangelist tells their own version of the same story: the life, death and resurrection of Jesus.
- Each gospel is written to meet the needs of a different Christian audience. For example: Matthew was written for those who had converted (changed) from

Judaism to Christianity; Luke was written for Gentiles (non-Jews) and emphasised the idea that Jesus was the saviour of all people.

The synoptics

The word synoptic means 'seen together'. The gospels of Mark, Matthew and Luke are referred to as the synoptics because they agree on:

- the main events of Jesus's life.
- the sequence in which these events occurred.
- the wording of Jesus's statements.

Mark was the first gospel to be written. The authors of Matthew and Luke both used Mark as a source when writing their own accounts. However, they also included material not found in Mark. Scholars believe that this other material came from the Q document.

> **key point**
>
> The name Q document comes from the German word *Quelle*, meaning 'source'. It is thought to have been a collection of Jesus's sayings, written some time between 50 and 64 CE. No copy of the Q document is known to have survived.

The Gospel of John

This was written after the synoptics, c. 90 CE. John differs from the synoptics in the following ways.

- It did not copy material from either Mark or the Q document.
- It does not mention the parables of Jesus and includes only a few of the miracle stories.
- It has a different sequence for certain events in Jesus's life. For example, John places the cleansing of the Temple early in Jesus's ministry, but the synoptics say it occurred later, during Holy Week.
- It is focused more on the question of Jesus's identity than on the events of his life. This is because by the end of the first century CE that was the question that most concerned Christians.

Stages in the development of the Gospels

Stage 1: The actual events in the life of Jesus. Jesus spent the three years of his public ministry communicating his message about the kingdom of God through parables, miracles and table fellowship. His disciples witnessed and remembered all of this.

Stage 2: The oral tradition of the early Christians. After the events of Easter and Pentecost, the disciples of Jesus began to preach his message far and wide. This was called the oral tradition because it was passed on by word of mouth from one person to another.

Stage 3: The written tradition of the early Christians. The original disciples who had witnessed Jesus's actions and words began to die out or were martyred. So the gospels were written in order to:

1. preserve important information about Jesus
2. correct any mistaken ideas about his teaching
3. provide readings for use in worship.

3 The Person and Preaching of Jesus

 aims

- To know what is involved in discipleship.
- To understand what Jesus meant about the Kingdom of God.
- To understand the role played by parables, miracles and table fellowship in Jesus's ministry.

Discipleship

To be a disciple of Jesus means learning from his example and continuing his mission.

key point

- Mission – carrying on the work of Jesus.
- Disciple – one who continues the mission of Jesus.

The New Testament teaches that becoming a disciple of Jesus demands a metanoia: a complete change of outlook that is demonstrated by making a total break from the way one has lived one's life and making a fresh start.

The Kingdom of God

Jesus's mission was to proclaim the Kingdom of God (also referred to as the Reign of God).

Difficulty

Jesus never offered a precise definition of the Kingdom of God. Instead, he used various images and stories to illustrate its meaning and inspire his listeners to think hard about what it meant and what it demanded of them.

Meaning

The Kingdom of God is not a place on the map. Jesus taught that:

- The Kingdom of God is in the **present**. Through the life and teaching of Jesus, the Kingdom of God has already come. It exists wherever God's love reigns in people's hearts and where they struggle to live their lives by God's standards.
- The Kingdom of God is **universal**, i.e. for all people, Jew and Gentile, male and female, rich and poor.
- The Kingdom of God is in the **future**. It exists as the ideal or perfect community in which people truly realise that they are all members of the one human family, and live lives committed only to goodness, justice and peace.
- The Kingdom of God is a very deep **mystery**. It is so profound that only God fully understands it. Although people can gain insight into it through prayer and good works, they can never hope to understand it fully.

The Beatitudes

- From the Latin word *beati* meaning 'happy' or 'blessed'.
- In the Beatitudes, Jesus set out the qualities people need if they want to become members of the Kingdom of God:
    1. deep faith in God
    2. detachment from wealth and property
    3. purity of heart
    4. willingness to forgive and be merciful
    5. commitment to peace.

The Kingdom of God made known through parables

Parable – a story that illustrates a message or point by using concrete examples drawn from everyday life.

The Parables				
Motive	Story-telling was an important part of Jewish culture and it was an effective way for Jesus to get his message across to people.			
Method	Jesus used images and examples drawn from farming, fishing and shepherding because these were activities his listeners were familiar with.			
Themes	The parables can be divided into four groups, each exploring an important theme in Jesus's teaching about the Kingdom of God.			
	1. Description of God.	2. How to behave in order to enter the Kingdom of God.	3. How people should treat one another in the Kingdom of God.	4. Warnings about the future day of judgment when God's Kingdom will come in all its fullness.
Examples	Prodigal Son	Talents	Good Samaritan	Weeds among the Wheat
Interpretation	A parable works on two levels: • on the surface – as an interesting, easily remembered story • at a deeper level – Jesus invites his listeners to work out the meaning hidden within a parable and apply its message to their lives.			

Example of a parable: The Good Samaritan

Luke 10:25–37

1. The story:

- This is the story of how a Samaritan man cared for a Jewish man whom he found injured and unconscious by the roadside.
- The injured man had been viciously attacked, robbed and left for dead.
- The Jewish man had been ignored by his fellow Jews, who passed by and left him to die.

- Then a Samaritan, travelling along the same road, saw the injured Jewish man and came to his aid.
- The Samaritan tended to his wounds, brought him to an inn and paid for him to be nursed back to health.

2. Explanation:

- The Samaritans were a people who lived in Samaria, the land between Judaea in the south of Palestine and Galilee in the north.
- Jews travelling between Judaea and Galilee would usually go across to the east bank of the river Jordan to avoid contact with the Samaritans.
- Samaritans were descended from Jews who had married foreigners (i.e. non-Jews) and there had been a quarrel between pure Jews and Samaritans for centuries.
- The Samaritans had built their own temple at Mount Gerazim and had their own version of the Tenakh.
- By the time of Jesus, most Jews despised the Samaritans and would have nothing to do with them.
- Jesus shocked his Jewish listeners by making a Samaritan the hero of this story. He did so to make important points about the Kingdom of God:

  1. There is no place for racial hatred or religious bigotry in God's kingdom.
  2. The neighbour whom God requires each person to love is anyone in need.

The Kingdom of God made known through miracles

Evidence for miracles

- The first-century Jewish historian Josephus referred to Jesus as a miracle-worker.
- The gospels record 35 different occasions when Jesus performed a miracle.

Miracle – a wonderful and awe-inspiring event that occurs solely as a result of God's direct action.

The four types of miracle

1. Healing miracles. *Example:* the Healing of a Paralytic.
2. Exorcisms (casting out demons). *Example:* the Gadarene Demoniac.
3. Nature miracles. *Example:* the Calming of a Storm.
4. Restorations to life. *Example:* the Raising of Jairus's daughter.

Example: A healing miracle (Luke 5:12–14)

- Jesus healed a man afflicted by leprosy.
- Lepers were social outcasts who were ordered to keep apart from other people because their disease was considered to be so contagious.

- By actually touching a person with leprosy, Jesus did something that no one else would have dared to do. He showed that while people may have rejected this man because of his illness, God had not.
- Jesus's actions revealed the love of God reaching out to and embracing people who were abandoned and suffering.

Need for miracles

Without clear evidence of Jesus's power over sin, suffering and death, his preaching about the Kingdom of God would have been dismissed by his Jewish audience.

This was because:

- Most Jews at that time saw physical suffering as a punishment from God for the sins one had committed.
- They would only believe that a person's sins had been forgiven if he/she was cured.
- By healing a person Jesus demonstrated that his authority to forgive sins and his power to heal came from God and that what he preached to them was true.

Jesus's motive for working miracles

- To strengthen the faith of those who already believed in him.
- To reveal God's power in order to show that the Kingdom of God had begun in him.
- To demonstrate God's unlimited love for each and every human being, regardless of their race or religion.

The Kingdom of God made known through table fellowship

- We often mark and celebrate important events in our lives by sharing a meal with family and friends.
- In first-century Palestine, a meal meant this and much more. Sharing a meal was a religious act. It formed an important part of the weekly celebration of the Sabbath. It symbolised unity and friendship.
- However, most Jews only shared a meal with people of the *same social class*.
- Jesus shocked people by sharing a meal with the outcasts of his society, e.g. tax collectors, such as Zacchaeus; and the poor, such as the five thousand he fed at Bethsaida.
- Jesus did this to show that the Kingdom of God is open to everyone – devout and sinner, Jew and Gentile.

4 The Passion, Death and Resurrection of Jesus

aims
- To understand the reasons for the conflict between Jesus and the Sanhedrin.
- To know about the events of Holy Week.

key point

- Passover – the annual celebration of the time when God sent Moses to free the Jews from slavery in Egypt. Also the time when most Jews believed the messiah would reveal himself.
- Martyrdom – suffering and dying for one's beliefs.
- Resurrection – the Christian belief that Jesus died on Good Friday and rose from the dead on Easter Sunday morning.
- Holy Week is the title given to the last week of Jesus's public ministry, set in spring, sometime during the years 30–33 CE.

The events of Holy Week

Sequence of Events	
Palm Sunday	Jesus arrives in Jerusalem seated on a colt (a humble animal of peace) and is welcomed by cheering crowds waving palm branches to salute him.
Monday	Jesus goes to the Temple and denounces the traders and money-changers who were cheating the pilgrims purchasing animals for sacrifice. He overturns their stalls and drives them out of the Temple. As a result of this, most of the Pharisees and the Sadducees in the Sanhedrin unite in a plot to kill Jesus.
Tuesday	Jesus teaches in the Temple and is asked some leading questions intended to trap him into criticising the Roman rule of Palestine and so provide a pretext for having him arrested.
Spy Wednesday	Judas Iscariot, one of Jesus's apostles, goes to the Jewish authorities and offers to betray Jesus so that he can be arrested quietly.
Holy Thursday	Jesus shares an evening meal with his disciples. This Passover meal is the first celebration of the eucharist. Judas leaves early. Later, in the Garden of Gethsemane, Judas arrives with the Temple police, who arrest Jesus.
Good Friday	During the early hours Jesus is interrogated by the Sanhedrin and later put on trial by the Roman procurator, Pontius Pilate. Jesus is scourged and condemned to death by crucifixion. He is nailed to an upright cross and suffers an agonising death. His body is buried in a nearby tomb hewn out of rock, which is then sealed by rolling a large boulder over its entrance.

Conflict with the Jewish authorities

Jesus and the Pharisees

- The Pharisees considered themselves the greatest experts on religious matters. While some Pharisees supported Jesus (e.g. Nicodemus and Joseph of Arimathea); most opposed him.
- Jesus had infuriated many Pharisees by criticising their legalism (harsh and excessive devotion to the precise letter of their religion's 613 laws).
- The Pharisees made the following accusations against Jesus.
  1. They said Jesus committed blasphemy by claiming to have the power to forgive sins.
  2. They said Jesus broke their religious laws by healing people on the Sabbath.
  3. They said Jesus was unfit to be called 'rabbi' because he mixed with sinners, outcasts and non-Jews.

Jesus and the Sadducees

- The Sadducees ignored Jesus until he directly challenged their authority by expelling the money-changers from the Temple's precincts.
- The Sadducees were embarrassed and furious with Jesus for doing this because, by publicly exposing the corrupt practices they had allowed to thrive in Judaism's holiest site, he had revealed their hypocrisy for all to see.

Consequences for Jesus

- Both the Pharisees and the Sadducees agreed that they could not allow Jesus to go on challenging their authority.
- Since Jesus could be neither intimidated nor bought off, they concluded that he had to be killed.

The arrest and trial of Jesus

- On Holy Thursday evening, Jesus was arrested and brought before the Sanhedrin. This was a court of inquiry and not a formal trial. It was not a fair hearing because Jesus was beaten and questioned in the hope that he would say something that would allow them to accuse him of an offence punishable by death.
- The High Priest, Caiaphas, asked Jesus directly if he was the messiah. When Jesus responded 'I am', his enemies condemned him for committing blasphemy.
- On Good Friday morning, a delegation from the Sanhedrin brought Jesus to the Antonia Fortress to be tried by the Roman procurator, Pontius Pilate.
- They claimed that Jesus was guilty of treason and should be executed because he had proclaimed himself to be the messiah and had threatened to lead a revolt.
- Pilate examined the evidence they offered and concluded that Jesus was innocent of these charges.

- Pilate believed that Jesus posed no threat to Roman rule but, in order to satisfy the Sanhedrin, he had Jesus scourged (flogged).
- When the Sanhedrin delegates still insisted on the death penalty, Pilate offered the crowd a choice between releasing Jesus or a violent rebel named Barabbas. To Pilate's surprise they chose to release Barabbas.

- When Pilate still hesitated to condemn Jesus, the Sanhedrin delegation threatened to report Pilate to the Emperor Tiberius for failing to execute an enemy of the empire.
- At this point Pilate gave in and ordered Jesus to be crucified.

The death and burial of Jesus

- Crucifixion was an agonising death.
- Jesus was forced to carry the wooden crossbeam to his place of execution on a hill outside the city walls – Golgotha (the place of the skull).
- He was nailed to the cross through his wrists and feet. Above his head a plaque was placed reading Jesus of Nazareth, King of the Jews.
- Jesus died from a combination of suffocation, exhaustion and blood loss.
- To ensure that Jesus was dead, Roman guards pierced his side with a spear, puncturing his lungs.
- Joseph of Arimathea claimed the body for burial. It was placed in a little tomb cut out of rock and located nearby.
- The tomb was sealed by rolling a large boulder across its entrance.

The resurrection of Jesus

Setting	Early on Easter Sunday morning a group of female disciples led by Mary Magdalene went to the tomb to embalm Jesus's corpse.
Discovery	They discovered that the stone covering the entrance had been rolled back and that the tomb was empty. Then they heard an announcement that Jesus had risen from the dead. Mary Magdalene met the risen Jesus in the garden nearby.
Reaction	The women went to tell the apostles, who were in hiding. At first the apostles did not believe them. Peter and John went to the tomb and found it empty. N.B.: the Gospels make it clear that no one actually witnessed Jesus rising from the dead. Their accounts deal with what occurred afterwards.
Appearances	Each appearance followed this pattern: • Jesus appeared among his disciples and reassured his astonished followers by saying, 'Peace be with you.' • Their initial shock faded and was replaced by an inner peace and joy. • He told them to 'Go and make disciples of all nations.'
Glorified	Jesus had not been restored to his former earthly life as had Lazarus. Jesus was/is no longer limited by the physical laws that limit all human actions. For example, Jesus could: • be physically present in two places at the same time • appear at will and disappear again. Through his resurrection Jesus was transformed and glorified (i.e. he lives a completely new, mysterious and higher form of life).

5 Faith in Jesus Christ

aims

HL
- To know about the development of the early Christian community.
- To understand the meaning of the titles of Jesus.

The Ascension

- Forty days after Easter Sunday, Jesus appeared to his disciples for one last time.
- He promised them that, although he would no longer be physically present among them, he would send the Holy Spirit to guide and strengthen them.

Pentecost

- Ten days later, the disciples gathered in Jerusalem to celebrate Pentecost (the Jewish harvest festival).
- The Holy Spirit came upon them 'like tongues of fire', giving them the courage and strength they would need to complete the work Jesus had begun.
- The disciples began publicly preaching that Jesus was the messiah and that he had risen, and began healing the sick in Jesus's name.
- The first Christian to be martyred was a deacon named Stephen, who was stoned to death in Jerusalem.

The story of St Paul

- The most outstanding Christian missionary (one who is sent to spread a religion) was Paul (or, in Hebrew, Saul) of Tarsus.
- Paul had been a devout Pharisee who had at one time persecuted Christians. However, while journeying from Jerusalem to Damascus, he had a vision that led him to convert to Christianity.
- Paul carried out three great missionary journeys around the eastern Mediterranean.
- During this time, he set up numerous new Christian communities.
- Paul wrote epistles (letters offering advice to his fellow Christians), which were later included in the New Testament.

- Paul was uniquely well-equipped for his mission because:
  - he was Jewish by religion
  - he had Roman citizenship
  - he spoke Aramaic, Greek, Hebrew and Latin, so he could communicate with both Jews and Gentiles.
- Paul was finally arrested by the Roman authorities and executed on the orders of Emperor Nero in 64 CE.

The Council of Jerusalem

- The first general council of Christian leaders was held in Jerusalem in 49 CE. It was called to decide a question that sharply divided Christians: did a person have to become a Jew before becoming a Christian?
- Paul won over Peter and the majority present to his solution: new converts did not have to become Jews before becoming Christians. All that was needed to become a Christian was repentance for one's sins, and baptism.
- This decision by the Council of Jerusalem severed Christianity's link with Judaism and established Christianity as a separate world religion.

The persecution of Christians

- By the mid-first century CE, the Roman authorities had grown highly suspicious of Christians for several reasons:
  1. Christians refused to acknowledge the emperor as a god or to worship him.
  2. They would not attend the bloodthirsty games in the arena and encouraged others to boycott them.
  3. They refused to enlist in the armed forces.
- When a fire destroyed much of the city of Rome in 64 CE, the Emperor Nero blamed the Christians. He launched a vicious persecution involving torture and crucifixion. Many Christians suffered martyrdom.
- Both Peter and Paul were put to death, along with hundreds of others. However, the Christian religion survived this and other periods of persecution.
- Finally, the Emperor Constantine granted Christians freedom of worship in 313 CE. By then, Christianity had spread as far as Ireland, Ethiopia, India and China.

(HL) The titles of Jesus

Messiah/Christ

The title Messiah comes from the Hebrew word *moshiach*, meaning someone who has been anointed or chosen by God to carry out an important task. When the Bible was first translated from Hebrew into Greek, the Greek word used in place of the Hebrew Messiah was *Christos*. From this we get the title Christ (also meaning 'anointed one').

Son of Man

This is the only title that Jesus is specifically recorded as having directly applied to himself. It comes from the Old Testament book of Daniel, where it was used to refer to the Messiah. Jesus claimed that he was the Son of Man because he could do things that only God could do, such as forgive people's sins.

Lord

For the Jews, God's name was Yahweh. However, they considered God's name so holy that it should never be spoken. Out of respect for God's name, the Jews substituted the title 'Lord' instead. The first Christians began to refer to Jesus as the Lord. This was because they believed that Jesus had authority over sin and power over death that belonged only to God.

Son of God

First-century Jews referred to an exceptionally good person as 'a son of God'. The early Christians reflected on Jesus's many references to God as his Father. From this they concluded that all Jesus had said and done had shown him to have a totally unique relationship with God. Jesus is not merely *a* son of God; he is *the* Son of God.

HL Past Exam Questions

Section 1 (All questions carry 5 marks each)

1. A historical source for the life of Jesus is:

   Jacob ☐ Job ☐ Josephus ☑ Joshua ☐

2. Galilee was a province in Palestine at the time of Jesus.

   True ☑ False ☐

3. The gospel of Luke is a synoptic gospel.

   True ☑ False ☐

4. Mark was the last gospel to be written.

   True ☐ False ☑

5. Discipleship means: _____

   _____

6. The governor of Palestine in the time of Jesus was Pontius Pilate.

   True ☑ False ☐

7. The Last Supper was a meal associated with which of the following religious celebrations?

   Bar Mitzvah ☐ Hanukkah ☐ Passover ☑ Sukkot ☐

8. According to the gospels, one person Jesus appeared to after his death and resurrection was __Mary Magdalene__

9. Christians call the coming of the Holy Spirit upon the disciples after the death of Jesus:

   Ascension ☐ Resurrection ☐ Pentecost ☑

10. One example of martyrdom from the founding story of Christianity is:

    __St Paul__

Section 2

1. This drawing is based on the miracle of Jesus raising Lazarus from the dead. (2006)

   A. Pick **one** thing from the drawing which shows how people reacted to the miracles of Jesus.

      _____

      _____

      _____ (2 marks)

   B. Name **one** other miracle that Jesus performed.

      _____ (4 marks)

   C. State **two** characteristics of the kingdom of God that can be seen in one of Jesus's miracles.

      _____

      _____ (4 marks)

2. This drawing is based on the Last Supper. (2007)

   A. Pick **one** thing from the drawing which shows that this is the Last Supper.

      _____

      _____

      _____

      _____

      (2 marks)

   B. On which of the following days of the week did Jesus celebrate the Last Supper? (Tick ✔ the correct box.)

      Wednesday ⬭   Thursday ✔   Friday ⬭   (2 marks)

   C. Give **two** reasons why the Last Supper was important for the first Christians.

      i. _____

      _____

      ii. _____

      _____

      (6 marks)

HL

3. This picture is based on the first Christians' experience of Pentecost. (2009)

A. Pick **one** thing from this picture which shows that it is based on the first Christians' experience of Pentecost.

_____

_____

_____

_____

(2 marks)

B. The first Christians experienced Pentecost after the death of Jesus. (Tick ✔ the correct box.)

True ☑   False ☐   (2 marks)

C. State **two** effects the experience of Pentecost had on the first Christians.

i. _____

_____

ii. _____

_____

(6 marks)

Section 4

1. (2009)

A.

(a) Name **one** parable that Jesus told his early followers. (5 marks)

(b) Outline **two** points that Jesus taught his followers about the Kingdom of God in a parable you have studied. (12 marks)

B.

(a) Explain **two** reasons why the Gospels are described as documents of faith. (18 marks)

(b) Outline what was involved in **three** different stages in the development of the Gospels. (15 marks)

2. (2008)

HL

A.

(a) Each of the different religious groups described below lived in Palestine at the time of Jesus. Tick ✔ the box that most correctly matches each description to the name of a religious group given below. The first description has been correctly matched to the name of a religious group as an example for you.

Religious group	The name of the religious group which matches this description is –(tick ✔ the correct box)	
1. We are wealthy aristocrats and have strong links with the Temple in Jerusalem. We accept Roman rule and have power in Palestine.	Pharisees	☐
	Sadducees	✔
	Zealots	☐
2. We reject Roman rule in Palestine and are ready to fight the Romans.	Pharisees	☐
	Sadducees	☐
	Zealots	✔
3. We do not co-operate with the Romans. We run the local synagogues and are strict about keeping all the laws of Judaism.	Pharisee	✔
	Sadducees	☐
	Zealots	☐

(8 marks)

(b) Pharisees ☐   Sadducees ☐   Zealots ☐

Choose **two** of the above groups and explain why each came into conflict with Jesus. (14 marks)

B.

(a) Give **two** reasons why the Sanhedrin was important in Palestine at the time of Jesus. (14 marks)

(b) Outline what happened when Jesus was brought before the Sanhedrin. (14 marks)

HL 3. (2007)

A.

Describe **one** incident from the life of Jesus that led to his death.   (15 marks)

B.

Outline **two** reasons why the incident you have described above led to the death of Jesus.   (20 marks)

C.

Outline how Jesus's death affected the people who were following him.   (15 marks)

4. (2006)

A.

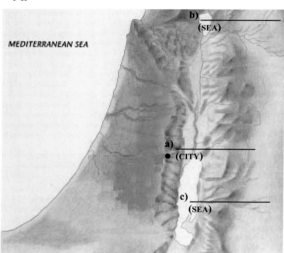

(a) In the spaces marked on this map of Palestine, write –

- The name of the city shown at (a)
- The names of the seas shown at (b) and (c).   (6 marks)

(b) Name an important event in the life of Jesus which happened in **one** of the places you have named above. (10 marks)

(c) Briefly outline what happened in the event you have named.   (10 marks)

B.

(a) Outline what the Jewish people expected the Messiah to be like at the time of Jesus.   (10 marks)

(b) Outline **one** way in which Jesus was like the Messiah that the Jewish people were expecting at the time.   (7 marks)

(c) Outline **one** way in which Jesus was not like the Messiah that the Jewish people were expecting at the time.   (7 marks)

Section 5

(Each question is worth 70 marks.)

1. Describe life in Palestine at the time of Jesus, referring to each of the following:
   i.   the political structures
   ii. the religious structures. (2009)

2. Outline **two** historical sources of information about the life of Jesus of Nazareth and discuss the ways in which they are similar to what the gospels say about his life and death. (2007)

3. Imagine you have been asked to give a talk at a Bible meeting explaining the stages involved in the development of the gospels from the oral tradition to the written word. Outline the talk you would give, making reference to the importance of the gospels in the Christian community of faith. (2004)

4. *In the parables Jesus tells people what the kingdom of God is like; in the miracles he shows people the kingdom of God among them.* – Mark Link

   Outline what is revealed about the kingdom of God in **one** parable and **one** miracle you have studied. (2005)

5. 'One of these two who became followers of Jesus after hearing what John had said was Andrew, the brother of Simon Peter. Early next morning, Andrew met his brother and said to him, "We have found the Messiah"- which means the Christ – and he took Simon to Jesus.' (John 1:40-42, *The Jerusalem Bible*)

   (a) Describe another incident from the Gospels when people used the title 'messiah' for Jesus.

   (b) Explain how the use of this title influenced the faith and practice of the early Christian community. (2003)

6. • Son of God   • Son of Man

   Outline what **one** of the above titles shows about the early Christians' understanding of Jesus.

SECTION C

Foundations of Religion: Major World Religions

- Cultural context – founding story of a particular religion.
- Founder(s) – the person(s) who started a religion.
- Sacred text – the holy book or scriptures of a particular religion.
- Ritual – a formal religious ceremony which recalls key events in the story of a religion and/or marks an important event in the life of a believer.
- Prayer – communication between human beings and God.
- Expansion – increase in the size of a religious community.

1 Judaism

aims

- To understand the meaning of Judaism.
- To know about the geographical and historical background to Judaism.

key point

- Patriarchs – the founding figures of Judaism: Abraham and Moses.
- Monotheism – the belief that there is only one God.
- Revelation – the way in which God makes his message known to human beings.

Context

The meaning of Judaism

- Judaism means the religion of the Jews (originally known as the Hebrews).
- Judaism is a monotheistic religion.

Geographical background

- Judaism originated in an area known as 'the Fertile Crescent', a narrow strip of land that stretches in an arc from the Persian Gulf in the east to Egypt in the west.
- Most of the story of the Jews took place in the area known today as the state of Israel and the Palestinian Territories.

Historical background

- Abraham said that God called him to lead his people out of Mesopotamia (modern Iraq) and bring them to the Promised Land (modern Israel).
- God made a covenant (sacred agreement) with Abraham and his descendants. If they faithfully worshipped God and kept God's laws, God would guarantee their ownership of the Promised Land.
- At first the Jews believed that each nation had its own god. In time they came to believe that there is only one God. Judaism became the world's first monotheistic religion.
- When famine struck the Promised Land (c. 1700 BCE), many Jews emigrated to Egypt. Although welcomed at first, they were later forced into slavery.
- After the Jews had suffered three centuries of oppression, God finally chose Moses to lead them to freedom.

- God spoke to Moses in the form of a bush that was on fire but was not burned up. He gave Moses the confidence to confront the Egyptian pharaoh and demand that he release the Jews.
- When the pharaoh refused, God sent a series of plagues, which forced him to set the Jews free.
- The great movement of the Jews back to the Promised Land is called the Exodus (the going forth).
- During this journey, God renewed his covenant with the Jews. If they were faithful to God's laws (summarised in the Ten Commandments given to Moses), God would once more guarantee their ownership of the Promised Land.
- Eventually, the Jews established the kingdom of Israel (meaning 'God strives') with its capital Jerusalem, where they built a temple to house the Ark of the Covenant (a casket containing the stone tablets on which the Ten Commandments were written).

Sources of evidence

- To know the name, origin and structure of Judaism's sacred text.

The Tenakh

Title

- The sacred text of Judaism is known as the Tenakh.
- This title comes from the initial letters of each of its three sections: T, N and K.

Origin

- Initially, important stories and doctrines were passed on by oral tradition (word of mouth) from one generation of Jews to the next.

Fragments of the Dead Sea Scrolls

- From about 1000 BCE onwards, these stories and doctrines were written down.

- Oldest known complete copy of the Tenakh – the Dead Sea Scrolls. These manuscripts were discovered in 1947, stored in clay jars hidden in caves in the Qumran wilderness near the Dead Sea in southern Israel.
- The scrolls had been hidden there in the mid-first century CE to prevent them being destroyed by the Romans.
- They may have been written by the Essenes.

Structure

- The Tenakh consists of 39 books, all written in Hebrew, which were gathered together into one volume.
- They can be divided into three groups: Torah; Nevi'im; and Ketuvim.

Section of the Tenakh	Meaning	Books	Contents/Message
Torah (or Pentateuch)	The Law	Genesis Exodus Leviticus Numbers Deuteronomy	The holiest part of the Tenakh because Moses received it direct from God. The story of the Jews from Abraham until their return to the Promised Land. Contains all the religious laws governing Jewish worship and daily life.
Nevi'im	The Prophets	Eight books	The story of the Jews after their return to the Promised Land.
Ketuvim	The Writings	Proverbs Psalms	Wise sayings Songs and poems praising God's goodness.

Beliefs, rites of passage and other rituals

- To know what Jews believe.
- To know how Jews practise their religion.

Jewish beliefs

God

- The Tenakh teaches that there is only one God, who is the all-knowing, all-powerful creator of the universe.
- The Hebrew name for God is Yahweh, but out of respect this name is not spoken. Instead, God is usually referred to as 'Adonai', meaning 'Lord'.

Covenant

- The covenant is the sacred agreement that God first made with Abraham and his descendants and later renewed with Moses and the Jews after their escape from Egypt.
- In it God promised the Jews that if they faithfully worshipped him and followed his laws, he would guarantee their ownership of the Promised Land.
- The symbol of this covenant is the ritual of male circumcision. This marks Jews as God's chosen people and reminds them of their duty to remain faithful to that covenant.

Prophets

- Jewish holy men who in ancient times received messages from God, which they then preached to their people.
- Famous prophets include Amos, Elijah, Jeremiah and Isaiah.
- They reminded the Jews of their duty to love God and follow his commandments.

Messiah

- Following their repeated conquest by foreign powers, the Jews were told by their prophets that God would send them a leader who would:
  1. be a descendent of King David
  2. free them from foreign domination
  3. restore Israel's greatness
  4. bring about an era of peace and prosperity.
- The leader chosen by God to fulfil this mission was given the title 'messiah' (meaning 'anointed one').
- Jews believe that the Messiah is yet to come.

Jewish symbols

Yarmulke

- A skullcap worn by Jewish men to demonstrate respect for God. It reminds Jews that God's wisdom is vastly greater than that of human beings.
- Most Jewish males wear the yarmulke because they believe that praying bareheaded shows a lack of respect for God.

A yarmulke

Tefillin

- Two cube-shaped leather boxes, each containing four passages from the Tenakh.
- One box is strapped to a Jewish man's forehead to remind him to think about what his religion teaches.
- The other box is tied around his upper forearm next to his heart to remind him to act on what his religion teaches.

Tallit

- A prayer shawl made of silk or wool. It is usually coloured blue and white and has fringes attached to its four corners as laid down in Numbers 15:37–41.
- The tallit is worn, draped across a man's shoulders, at morning prayers only.

Tefillin

Mezuzah

- Jews consider the home to be a sacred place. The most visible symbol of this is the mezuzah.
- It is a small decorated container, which is fixed to the upper third of most doorposts in Jewish homes.
- The mezuzah contains the verses of the Shema (Deuteronomy 6:4–9).

A mezuzah

- Jews touch the mezuzah when entering or leaving a room to remind themselves of their Jewish beliefs and identity.

Jewish worship

- According to the Torah, God commanded that the seventh day of the week should be a day of worship and relaxation.
- Jews refer to the seventh day as Shabbat or the Sabbath day.
- Shabbat begins at sunset on Friday and ends at nightfall on Saturday.
- Many Jews believe that all business activities, shopping and the use of most technology should be avoided on the Shabbat.
- Jews may attend a service in the synagogue on Saturday morning or on the previous Friday evening. The service consists of:

1. readings from the Torah

2. prayers and hymns

3. a sermon on the readings.

- Faithful observance of the Shabbat is considered vitally important as it encourages Jews to keep the covenant God made with their ancestors.

The Jewish place of worship

A synagogue

- Jews worship in a synagogue. The word synagogue comes from the Greek word *synagein*, meaning 'to gather together'.

- A synagogue is a simple rectangular building, which serves three purposes:

  1. a house of prayer where services are held each Shabbat and on festival days

  2. a place of education where children learn Hebrew and study the Tenakh

  3. a community centre for meetings of various Jewish organisations.

- The synagogue became the centre of Jewish community life after the destruction of the Temple in 70 CE and the dispersion of the Jewish people out of Palestine that followed this.

- Some features of the synagogue recall aspects of the Temple:

  1. its layout is based on the Temple

  2. it faces towards Jerusalem, where the Temple once stood

  3. the Ner Tamid (perpetual lamp) represents the Menorah (seven-branched candlestick) which was always lit in the Temple.

- In traditional synagogues, men and women sit separately.

Jewish rituals

Initiation (Naming and circumcision)

- Children are considered a blessing and a gift from God.

- Eight days after a boy is born, he is formally named at a ceremony held in the local synagogue.

- The name chosen has a meaning, e.g. Isaiah (God is salvation); Joshua (Saviour).

- On the same day the ritual of Brit Milah (the covenant of the circumcision) takes place.

- Circumcision involves the removal of the loose foreskin over the penis. This operation is carried out by a mohel (a man specially trained for this task).

- Circumcision is taught to be necessary for all male Jews because it is believed to have been demanded by God when he made his covenant with Abraham.
- A Jewish girl is usually given her name on the first Shabbat after her birth.
- In reformed and liberal Jewish communities, a girl is given her name when she is seven days old in a ceremony called Zeved Habat (which means 'gift of a daughter').

Initiation into adulthood (Bar Mitzvah/Bat Mitzvah)

- Boys are declared adults at the age of 13. The Bar Mitzvah (Son of the Commandments) is a ceremony held to mark a boy's new status as an adult.
- Judaism recognises that girls generally mature earlier than boys, and girls are considered adults at the age of 12.
- The Bat Mitzvah (Daughter of the Commandments) is a ceremony held by Jews in reformed and liberal communities to mark a girl's new status as an adult.
- Both boys and girls spend several years preparing for the ceremony. They must learn Hebrew so that they can read from the Torah in the synagogue.
- In these ceremonies young Jews commit themselves to living out their beliefs faithfully in their daily lives.
- A celebratory meal is held after the ceremony.

Jewish religious festivals

- Rosh Hashanah – marks start of Jewish New Year.
- Yom Kippur – 24-hour period of fasting hours when Jews seek God's forgiveness.
- Sukkot (Tabernacles) – commemorates how God cared for Jews as they travelled through the desert to the Promised Land.
- Hanukkah (Festival of Lights) – commemorates the re-dedication of the Temple in 165 BCE and celebrates the survival of Judaism in spite of great persecution. Held in winter.
- Shavuoth – feast celebrating God giving the Ten Commandments to Moses.
- Pesach (Passover) – seven-day festival in Israel; eight days elsewhere. Commemorates God freeing the Jews from captivity in Egypt. High point of this festival is the Seder (Passover meal).

Passover and the Seder

The Seder is the Jewish ritual meal held to celebrate the annual Feast of Passover. It follows this pattern:

1. In preparation for the Seder, Jewish families remove all traces of hametz (leavened/yeast bread) from homes. Special plates, glassware and cutlery that have had no contact with yeast bread are used.
2. The Seder begins with the head of the household saying a prayer called the Kiddush. Everyone takes parsley which has been dipped in salt water. The head of the household then breaks the matzah (a loaf of unleavened bread) and shares it out among those present.

3. During the meal, wine is drunk with the food: one glass of wine is poured but left untouched. This symbolises (represents) the belief that, at some future time, the prophet Elijah will return and announce the arrival of the Messiah.

4. The youngest person present then asks: 'Why is this night different from all other nights?' The head of the household responds by reading the story of the Passover and the Exodus, telling of how God freed their ancestors from slavery in Egypt.

Development of tradition

aims

- To know the key events in the story of the Jewish people.
- To understand Jewish dietary laws.
- To know the story of the Jewish community in Ireland.

Key events in the story of Judaism

key point

- The destruction of the Temple in Jerusalem (70 CE) following a failed Jewish revolt in Palestine against their Roman overlords.

- The diaspora (dispersion) of the Jewish people from Palestine to other parts of the world following the destruction of the Temple.

- Pogroms (regular, organised persecutions) against the Jews who formed a small minority in a Europe.

- The Holocaust – the systematic, state-sponsored murder of six million Jews committed by the Nazis between 1938 and 1945.

- In 1948, the state of Israel was established as a homeland for the Jewish people.

- Commitment – dedication and loyalty to something.
- Persecution – oppression, injury and death inflicted on a group.

The flag of the modern state of Israel

Jewish dietary laws

- All Jews are expected to follow a special diet.
- Kashrut is the name given to the laws set out in Leviticus 17, which state:
    1. what can be eaten by Jews
    2. what they are forbidden to eat
    3. how permitted foods should be prepared.
- Permitted food is referred to as kosher. *Examples*: fish with fins and scales; meat from animals that both chew the cud and have cloven (split) hooves.

- Pigs have cloven hooves but do not chew the cud, so Jews are not permitted to eat pig meat.
- All animals deemed kosher must be killed according to the rules of shechita. This involves slitting the animal's throat with only one cut so as to minimise its pain. Then the animal is entirely drained of its blood.
- Separate utensils must always be used when preparing meat and dairy products.
- Jews believe that faithfully following the laws concerning food helps to preserve their distinct religious identity and encourages them to obey all God's laws.

The Jewish community in Ireland

- The earliest documentary evidence mentions the arrival of five Jewish merchants in Ireland in the eleventh century.
- By the beginning of the sixteenth century, a small number of Jews had settled in the Munster region after they were expelled from Portugal.
- In 1555, William Annyas was elected Mayor of Youghal, Co. Cork. By the 20th century, Jews were participating fully in all walks of life.
- Robert Briscoe was twice elected Lord Mayor of Dublin (1956 and 1961), an achievement repeated by his son Ben in 1988. Gerald Goldberg became Lord Mayor of Cork in 1977.
- The earliest record of a synagogue in Ireland dates from 1660.
- The Jewish population in Ireland peaked at 5,500 in the late 1940s. Today it stands at about 1,700.

Tradition, faith and practice today

aims
- To understand the structure of the Jewish community.
- To know about the divisions within Judaism.

The Jewish community worldwide

- There are an estimated 18 million Jews worldwide.
- Approximately 25 per cent live in Israel and 30 per cent in the USA.

key point

Tradition – **passing on long-held beliefs and practices from one generation to the next.**

Important figures in the Jewish community

- Rabbi – see information on page 14.
- Cantor (chazan) – leads the congregation in singing the hymns and chanting prayers during services in the synagogue.
- Shochet – Jewish butcher trained in methods of slaughtering and cooking animals according to kashrut.

Divisions within Judaism

Modern Judaism has four main branches:

- Orthodox
- Reform
- Conservative
- Hasidic.

Orthodox Judaism

Orthodox Jews see themselves as the only faithful practitioners of the ancient religion of Israel. Orthodox Jews are required to:

1. follow strictly the 613 mitzvot (commandments) of the Torah
2. accept the interpretation of these mitzvot as set down in the Talmud (ancient commentary on the Torah)
3. conduct all religious services in Hebrew
4. strictly observe all the religious rituals (festivals and rites of passage).

Orthodox Jews also insist that:

1. women and men must be seated separately during worship in the synagogue
2. women cannot become rabbis.

Reform Judaism

- The Reform tradition in Judaism began in Europe in the late 18th century.
- Reform Jews believe that the Torah should be interpreted to take into account the changes that have occurred since it was first written.
- Reform Jews have relaxed and changed certain laws relating to worship in the synagogue to suit modern life. For example:
    1. men and women can sit together during worship in the synagogue
    2. girls undergo the bat mitzvah (equivalent to the bar mitzvah for boys)
    3. women may be ordained as rabbis.

Conservative Judaism

- Conservative Judaism began in North America in the 1940s.
- Its members seek a middle way between the Orthodox and Reform types of Judaism.
- Conservative Jews hold firmly to all the essential traditions of Judaism while at the same time accepting certain elements of the Reform approach.
- For example:
    1. they interpret the Torah in a way that meets the realities of modern society
    2. they ordain women as rabbis.

Hasidic Judaism

- Hasid means 'pious (dutiful) one'.
- The Hasidic movement in Judaism was started in the eighteenth century by Rabbi Israel Baal Shem Tov (d. 1760).
- Hasidic Jews have a very distinctive style of dress. Men grow long beards and long curling locks of hair either side of their heads. They wear distinctive black clothing and wide-brimmed hats.
- The Hasidic tradition:

  1. demands literal faithfulness to the words of the Torah

  2. places more emphasis on the enthusiastic praise of God than on scholarship

  3. teaches that its leaders (called rebbe) have greater insight than rabbis into religious matters.

An Hasidic Jew

2 Islam

aims
- To understand the meaning of Islam.
- To know about the geographical and historical background to Islam.

Context

The meaning of Islam

- Islam means 'peace through submission' to the revealed will of Allah.
- Muslim (a follower of Islam) means 'one who submits'.

Geographical background

The city of Makkah (Mecca) in the Arabian peninsula (modern Saudi Arabia).

Historical background

- Muhammad (the name means 'highly praised') was born in Makkah around 570 CE.
- He became a successful businessman and a highly respected figure in Makkah. People called him Al-Amin, which means 'the trustworthy one'.
- Muhammad grew increasingly troubled by the corruption and injustice he saw around him. He spent many hours praying and fasting alone in a cave on Mount Hira.
- On the Night of Power and Excellence in 610 CE, the archangel Gabriel is said to have appeared and told Muhammad that he would be the Prophet of Allah – the one who would tell people the will of God.
- In 613 CE Muhammad received another revelation, and began publicly preaching in Makkah. He said that people should:
  1. abandon polytheism
  2. believe in Allah
  3. treat one another fairly
  4. care for the sick and poor.
- Muhammad demanded that all idols should be removed from the Kaaba ('the House of God'). He said that the Kaaba should be used exclusively for the worship of Allah.
- However, these idols attracted many pilgrims to Makkah and the city's businessmen saw Muhammad as a threat to the huge profits that they were making from these pilgrims.
- Mohammad and his followers suffered increasing persecution as a result of his demand.

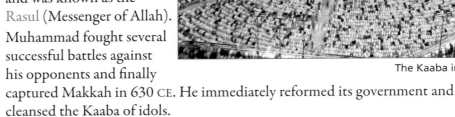

- In 622 CE Muhammad and his followers left Makkah and moved to Madinah ('city of the prophet'). This event is known as the Hijrah or Hegira ('the departure').
- In time, Muhammad became ruler of Madinah and was known as the Rasul (Messenger of Allah).
- Muhammad fought several successful battles against his opponents and finally

The Kaaba in Makkah

captured Makkah in 630 CE. He immediately reformed its government and cleansed the Kaaba of idols.
- By 631 CE Islam had spread across all of Arabia. Muhammad fell ill and died the following year.

Sources of evidence

- To know the name, origin and structure of Islam's sacred text.

Title	Date	Structure	Content
The Qur'an (pronounced 'Koran'), means 'that which is to be read'.	Mid-seventh century CE.	114 surahs (chapters), written in Arabic.	1. Basic beliefs of Islam. 2. Clear and strict guidelines about how Muslims should live. 3. Punishments for wrongdoing.

Muslims believe that the Qur'an is literally the word of God. They are taught to treat every copy of the Qur'an with great respect: for example, it should be handled with care and never left lying on the ground.

Beliefs, rites of passage and other rituals

- To understand key Islamic beliefs.
- To know how Muslims practise their religion.

Islamic beliefs

The key doctrines of Islam are known as the five articles of faith.

1. There is only one God, who is named Allah.
2. Angels are Allah's messengers.
3. The Qur'an is the final and complete revelation of Allah.
4. Muhammad is the last and the greatest prophet of Allah.
5. There will be a final day of judgment, when Allah will reward the good and punish the wicked.

The five pillars of faith

Muslims are obliged to uphold their beliefs by practising the five pillars of faith.

1st Pillar	Shahadah	To recite the following creed five times each day: 'There is no God but Allah, and Muhammad is his prophet.'
2nd Pillar	Salat	To pray at set times each day and to attend a mosque for communal prayer on Friday.
3rd Pillar	Zakat	To give alms (charity) to the poor, either voluntarily or by state deduction, of one-fortieth of one's earnings.
4th Pillar	Sawm	To fast during the daylight hours of Ramadan.
5th Pillar	Hajj	To go on pilgrimage to Makkah at least once in one's lifetime.

The Islamic place of worship

Muslims worship in a mosque, which means 'a place of prostration'. A mosque serves two functions:

1. a place where Allah is worshipped
2. a centre for the education of Muslim children.

Interior and exterior of a mosque

KEY FEATURES OF A MOSQUE

1. Minaret – the tower from which the muezzin (crier) calls Muslims to prayer.
2. Minbar – a raised platform from which the imam gives the sermon and leads prayers.
3. Mihrab – an alcove in a wall that points towards Makkah.
4. Communal prayer – everyone sits in rows on the floor to emphasise the belief that everyone is equal before Allah. However, men and women pray in separate areas.
5. Wudu area – where ritual washing is carried out before worship begins.
6. Decoration – mosques are decorated only with calligraphy and geometric designs. The Qur'an forbids the drawing or painting of any image of Allah, which would be shirk (blasphemy).

Islamic ritual of initiation (Naming)

- The birth of a child is regarded as barakah: a blessing from Allah.
- Aqiqa is the Muslim naming ceremony.
  Seven days after the birth the ritual of Aqiqa is held.
    1. The child's head is shaved and its weight in gold or silver is given to the poor.
    2. The parents make a sacrifice to give thanks for the child – two sheep if it is a boy and one sheep if it is a girl. One-third of the sacrifice is given to the poor.
    3. The child is named, either after Muhammad or one of his family, or with a name that has a religious meaning (e.g. Abdullah, which means Servant of Allah).
- Boys are usually circumcised, although this sometimes occurs in a separate ceremony at the age of seven.

The Islamic calendar

- The Islamic calendar follows the lunar cycle (the time between one full moon and the next). As a result, the Muslim year is eleven days shorter than that of Jews and Christians.
- Muslims date their era from 622 CE, the year Muhammad emigrated from Makkah to Madinah.
- Eid or id is the Arabic word for festival.
- An Islamic festival is a large-scale communal celebration designed to encourage friendship and goodwill. Gifts are exchanged and traditionally food is donated to the poor.

Islamic religious festivals

- Hijrah – marks beginning of Muslim year. Recalls Muhammad leaving Makkah and going to Madinah.
- Ramadan – commemorates Muhammad receiving the Qur'an from Allah. People fast during daylight hours.

- Eid ul-Fitr – celebrates end of Ramadan.
- Eid ul-Adha – held in final month of Muslim year. A four-day festival that celebrates completion of the Hajj.

Pilgrimage in Islam

- The pilgrimage to Makkah, Islam's holiest place, is known as the Hajj.
- It is the duty of every Muslim to make this journey at least once in their lifetime.
- Those who participate in the Hajj in a spirit of reverence will have their sins forgiven. Those who die while journeying either to or from Makkah are declared martyrs and immediately welcomed into paradise by Allah.
- On arrival in Makkah all pilgrims bathe and men put on the ihram (a white cotton garment) to symbolise the equality of all men before Allah.

THE PILGRIMAGE ROUTE

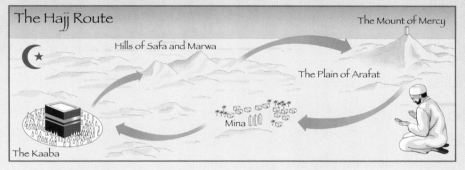

The Hajj Route

The Mount of Mercy

Hills of Safa and Marwa

The Plain of Arafat

Mina

The Kaaba

1. Muslim pilgrims walk around the Kaaba seven times in an anti-clockwise direction. They kiss/touch the black stone in the centre.
2. They pass seven times between the hills of Safa and Marwa and drink from the Zamzam (well).
3. They go to the Plain of Arafat and pray from noon to dusk.
4. They go to Mina and throw stones at the three pillars to symbolise their rejection of the Devil.
5. Then they return to Makkah and walk seven times around the Kaaba.

Development of tradition

aims

- To know the key events in the story of Islam.
- To know the story of the Muslim community in Ireland.

Key events in the story of Islam

- Muhammad died in 632 CE. Within a century of his death, Islam had spread as far as Spain to the west and India to the east.
- Following Muhammad's death, the rival factions among his followers agreed to choose a caliph (successor to Muhammad).
- The first caliph was Abu Bakr, the father of Muhammad's youngest wife.

Later, a bitter dispute broke out about how the caliph should be chosen. Two groups formed:

1. the Sunni (orthodox) Muslims, who accepted the next caliph
2. the Shia (Shi'at Ali, or Party of Ali), who rejected the next caliph and followed the descendents of Ali, Muhammad's son-in-law.

The Islamic community in Ireland

- There are mosques in Dublin, Cork, Galway and Belfast.
- The first mosque in Ireland, opened in 1975, was in Harrington Street, Dublin.
- The first Muslim national school (primary level) was opened in 1990 and moved to its current site at Clonskeagh, Dublin in 1993.
- In 1992, Dr Moosajee Bhamjee became the first Muslim to be elected to the Oireachtas as a TD for Co. Clare.

Dr Moosajee Bhamjee, the first Muslim TD

- The Islamic Cultural Centre was opened at Clonskeagh in 1996.

HL Tradition, faith and practice today

aims

- To understand the global nature of the Islamic community.
- To know about the divisions within Islam.

The Islamic community worldwide

- Islam is the world's second largest and fastest growing religion. It has an estimated 1.3 billion members worldwide.
- The majority of Muslims (about 90 per cent) are Sunni; the remainder are Shia.
- Shias are the dominant group in Iran and Pakistan.
- Islam's three holiest sites are Makkah, Madinah and Jerusalem.

The divisions within Islam

There has been a deep rift within Islam since the assassination of Ali in 661 CE. Two factions developed over how the caliph should be chosen:

1. The Sunnis wanted to chose a leader purely on the basis of his qualities and ability to do the task.
2. The Shias claimed that only a blood relative of Muhammad was acceptable as caliph.

They also disagree on the text of the Qur'an:

1. Sunnis believe that today's Qur'an is a faithful and unaltered copy of the original.
2. Many Shias believe that the Qur'an was altered by the Sunnis, who removed any verses from the text that supported the Shia position.

3 Buddhism

aims
- To understand the meaning of Buddhism.
- To know about the geographical and historical background of Buddhism.

Context

The meaning of Buddhism

- Buddhism is a set of beliefs based on the teachings of the Buddha.
- Buddha is a title that means 'The enlightened one'. It was given to the founder of Buddhism – Siddhartha Gautama.

Geographical background

Buddhism began in the foothills of the Himalayan Mountains, on the borders of modern India and Nepal.

Historical background

- Siddhartha Gautama (c. 565–483 BCE) was a Hindu prince who enjoyed a luxurious and sheltered lifestyle until he became an adult.
- When Siddhartha began travelling throughout northern India, what he saw deeply shocked him.
  1. On his first journey he met an old man and learned about old age.
  2. On his second journey he met a man covered in sores and learned about illness.
  3. On his third journey he saw a corpse about to be cremated and learned about death.
  4. On his fourth journey he met a wandering ascetic who taught him that true happiness cannot be achieved either by amassing great wealth or by the pursuit of pleasure.
- These four experiences, which profoundly changed Siddhartha's whole outlook on life, are called the Four Sights.
- Siddhartha decided to devote the rest of his life to finding answers to life's great questions.
- On the Blessed Night of the Great Renunciation he rejected his royal status by taking on the identity of a beggar and left his palace, never to return.

key point

Ascetic: A person who leads a very simple life and abstains from normal life pleasures.

- For the next five years, Siddartha lived as a wandering ascetic.
- On his thirty-fifth birthday he sat beneath a banyan tree and meditated on all that he had experienced and learned. After three nights he gained enlightenment: a deep understanding of the meaning of life.
- He then travelled to Benares, a city on the River Ganges, where he began preaching his message and made many converts. His followers gave him the title Buddha ('Enlightened One').

Sources of evidence

- To know the name, origin and structure of Buddhism's sacred text.

Name

- The sacred text of Buddhism is the Pali Canon.
- Pali is an ancient northern Indian language, which may have been spoken by the Buddha. 'Canon' means 'an agreed set of writings'.

Date

- Written in the first century BCE by Buddhist monks and nuns in Sri Lanka.
- They recorded the stories and sayings of the Buddha, which had been passed on orally for several centuries.

Structure

The Pali Canon consists of 45 volumes divided into three sections known as the Tripitaka (the Three Baskets):

Vinaya	Discipline Basket	Rules for the Sangha (Buddhist community of monks and nuns).
Sutta	Instruction Basket	Buddha's sermons.
Abhidhamma	Great Teaching Basket	Analyses of Buddha's most profound and important teachings.

Beliefs, rites of Passage and other Rituals

- To understand key Buddhist beliefs.
- To know how Buddhists practise their religion.

Buddhist beliefs

Reincarnation

Human beings must undergo reincarnation – a long cycle of birth, death and rebirth.

Karma

Everything people think, say and do in this life has an impact on their future lives.

- If we do something good it creates positive karma.
- If we do something bad it creates negative karma.

Nirvana

It is only when people accumulate enough positive karma that they can be freed from the cycle of reincarnation and achieve nirvana – the state of complete happiness and perfect peace.

The four noble truths

People can only achieve nirvana by accepting the four noble truths.

1. All life is dukkha (suffering).
2. Dukkha is caused by desire (wanting things).
3. Dukkha can only be overcome by ceasing to desire.
4. This can only be achieved by following the Eightfold Path.

The Eightfold Path

These are the eight steps one must follow to end dukkha and achieve nirvana.

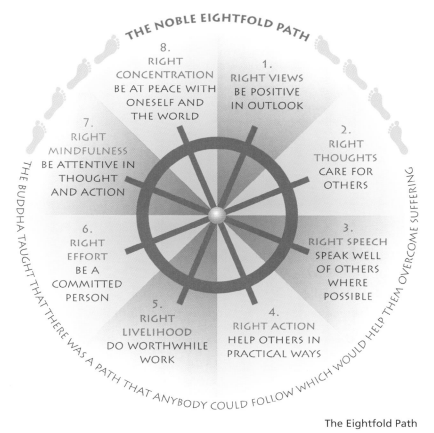

THE NOBLE EIGHTFOLD PATH

8. RIGHT CONCENTRATION BE AT PEACE WITH ONESELF AND THE WORLD

1. RIGHT VIEWS BE POSITIVE IN OUTLOOK

7. RIGHT MINDFULNESS BE ATTENTIVE IN THOUGHT AND ACTION

2. RIGHT THOUGHTS CARE FOR OTHERS

6. RIGHT EFFORT BE A COMMITTED PERSON

3. RIGHT SPEECH SPEAK WELL OF OTHERS WHERE POSSIBLE

5. RIGHT LIVELIHOOD DO WORTHWHILE WORK

4. RIGHT ACTION HELP OTHERS IN PRACTICAL WAYS

THE BUDDHA TAUGHT THAT THERE WAS A PATH THAT ANYBODY COULD FOLLOW WHICH WOULD HELP THEM OVERCOME SUFFERING

The Eightfold Path

Buddhist symbols

- Light – symbolises the wisdom that drives away the darkness caused by ignorance and prejudice.
- Incense – its fragrance symbolises the moral purity that each person should strive to achieve.
- Flowers – a reminder that all things pass away and that people should not pointlessly strive to fill their lives with material possessions.

Buddhist place of worship

A Buddhist temple is usually a part of a sangha, a monastery where Buddhist monks and nuns live as a community.

A Buddhist temple

Key Features of a Buddhist Temple	
Temple complex	A shrine room, meditation rooms and teaching halls. Buddhists remove their shoes before entering as a mark of respect.
Statue of Buddha	Situated in the shrine room. Shown sitting in lotus (meditation) position to symbolise enlightenment. Buddhists recite the three refuges, bow three times before the statue, then burn candles and incense to create positive karma.
Bell and drum	The bell is rung and the drum beaten during festival times. Smaller bells inside the shrine room are rung during daily devotions.

Buddhist festivals

Wesak

- Celebrates the birth, enlightenment and death of the Buddha. Held in May, or in June during a leap year.
- Lay people visit temples and light candles to symbolise Buddha's enlightenment. Gifts are exchanged and parties are organised for children.

Kathina

- The festival of giving that occurs at the end of Asalha (the rainy season). It follows three months of quiet meditation for monks and nuns.
- The members of a sangha ask each other for forgiveness for any ways in which they have offended each other.

- Lay people go to the sanghas and offer practical gifts (e.g. food and cloth for making robes) to the monks and nuns.

Buddhist places of pilgrimage

Buddhists believe that going on pilgrimage creates positive karma and so helps them to achieve a better life following their next reincarnation.

The two most important Buddhist places of pilgrimage are:

1. Bodh Gaya in Bihar, where the Buddha achieved enlightenment.
2. Sarnath in Uttar Pradesh, where he gave his first sermon.

Many Buddhists try to visit a place associated with the Buddha, such as the Tooth Relic Temple in Kandy, Sri Lanka. This is said to have housed the Buddha's teeth since they were brought there in the fourth century BCE.

Development of tradition

- To understand how two strands developed within Buddhism.
- To know the story of Buddhism in Ireland.

The two strands in Buddhism

Theravada

- Theravada means 'the way of the elders'. It is the oldest school of Buddhist thought.
- It is found in Burma, Cambodia, Laos, Sri Lanka and Thailand.
- Its followers believe that:
    1. the Buddha was a great and holy man, but not a god.
    2. the only authentic source of guidance on how to achieve nirvana is to be found in the Pali Canon.
    3. only monks and nuns can achieve enlightenment.

Mahayana

- This means 'the great vehicle'. Most of the world's Buddhists belong to this group.
- It is found in China, Japan, Korea and Vietnam.
- Its members (influenced by Hinduism) believe that:
    1. the Buddha was a god. They worship him in elaborate rituals.
    2. there are Bodhisattvas – people who have already achieved enlightenment but chose to remain on earth to help others achieve nirvana.
    3. nirvana can be achieved by everyone, not just monks and nuns.

Buddhism in Ireland

- The first Buddhist centre in Ireland, Kagyu Samye Dzong, was established in 1977 at Kilmainham, Dublin.
- Dzogchen Beara Retreat Centre was later set up in West Cork.
- Both offer instruction in meditation and the Buddhist way of life.

 # Tradition, faith and practice today

> **aims** • To know about the distribution and expansion of Buddhism.

Buddhism today

- Buddhism is the world's fourth largest religion. It has an estimated membership of 350 million worldwide.
- Buddhism is the majority religion in Sri Lanka and the state religion of Bhutan and Thailand.
- Thanks to the missionary efforts of King Asoka of Sri Lanka (third century BCE), there are now substantial Buddhist populations all across southern Asia.
- In recent times Buddhism has gained many new converts in China (since the death of Chairman Mao) and in India (among the Untouchables).
- Buddhism has spread outside Asia and has begun to attract a small but growing membership in Western Europe.

Past Exam Questions

Section 1 (All questions carry 5 marks each)

1. Abraham is most associated with which world religion?

   Buddhism ⬭   Hinduism ⬭   Judaism ⬭

2. In a major world religion, a prophet is someone who reveals the will of God.

   True ⬭   False ⬭

3. Muslims believe in one God, whom they call:

   Allah ⬭   Buddha ⬭   Yahweh ⬭

4. The name of the Buddha is _____

5. A mosque is a place of worship associated with Judaism.

   True ⬭   False ⬭

6. The law of karma is associated with Islam.

   True ⬭   False ⬭

7. Bar Mitzvah is a festival in which world religion?

   _____

8. Zakat is an important part of the moral code of Islam.

   True ⬭   False ⬭

9. The Hajj is a journey made by devout followers of:

   Islam ⬭   Christianity ⬭   Buddhism ⬭

10. The Eightfold Path is most associated with which of the following world religions?

    Buddhism ⬭   Islam ⬭   Judaism ⬭

Section 2

1. This is a photograph of people taking part in a religious pilgrimage.

   A. Pick **one** thing from this photograph which shows that these people are taking part in a pilgrimage.

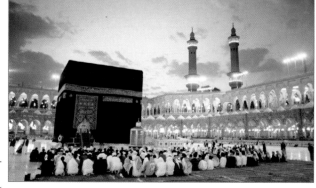

   _____

   _____

   _____ (2 marks)

HL

B. Buddhism ⬭ Islam ⬭ Judaism ⬭

Tick ✔ **one** of the above world religions and name a place of pilgrimage associated with it.

_____ (2 marks)

C. State **two** reasons why members of a world religion would take part in a pilgrimage.

i. _____

_____

ii. _____

_____

(6 marks)

2. This is a photograph of people practising their religion.

A. Pick **one** thing from this photograph which shows that these people are practising their religion.

_____

_____

_____

(2 marks)

B. Give **one** reason why people practise their religion in this way.

_____

(2 marks)

C. State **two** other ways in which people can practise their religion.

i. _____

_____

ii. _____

_____

(6 marks)

Section 4

1. (2009)

A.

Buddhism ⬭   Hinduism ⬭   Islam ⬭   Judaism ⬭

Tick ✔ **one** of the major world religions above that you have studied.

(a) Name **one** part of the world associated with the founding story of the major world religion you have ticked above.

_____ (5 marks)

(b) Describe the way people lived in the part of the world you have named above at the time the world religion began. (20 marks)

B.

(a) Read the list of religious titles and the list of world religions given below. One religious title has been matched to the world religion with which it is most associated as an example for you. Make **one** other match.

Religious Titles	World Religions
Brahmin	Buddhism
Rabbi	Christianity
Imam	Hinduism
Monk	Islam
Priest	Judaism

Example:

Priest	Christianity

Answer:

(5 marks)

(b) • Buddhism   • Hinduism   • Islam   • Judaism

Outline the way in which the community is structured in **one** of the major world religions listed above. (20 marks)

2. (2008)

A.

Tick ✔ **one** of the following major world religions you have studied.

Buddhism ⬭   Hinduism ⬭   Islam ⬭   Judaism ⬭

(a) People of faith gather to mark key moments in life such as birth, death etc. Name **one** religious ceremony that marks an important moment in the life of a believer in the world religion you have ticked above. (5 marks)

(b) Outline what happens during the religious ceremony you have named above. (20 marks)

HL

B.

(a) State the name given to the building where members of the world religion you have ticked above regularly gather for prayer.

(b) Describe **two** ways in which the place you have named above helps believers to pray. (20 marks)

3. (2007)

A.

Buddhism ⬭ Hinduism ⬭ Islam ⬭ Judaism ⬭

Tick ✔ **one** of the world religions above that you have studied.

(a) Name **one** key person/group of people associated with the founding story of the world religion you have ticked above.

_____ (5 marks)

(b) Explain why the person/group of people you have named is important in the founding story of the world religion you have ticked above. (10 marks)

B.

Outline **one** way in which the story of the earliest followers influences members today in the world religion you have ticked above. (15 marks)

C.

Explain how the world religion you have ticked above is linked to another major world religion. (20 marks)

4. (2006)

A.

(a) Tick ✔ **one** of the following world religions you have studied and name the sacred text associated with it:

Buddhism ⬭ Hinduism ⬭ Islam ⬭ Judaism ⬭

Name of sacred text: _____ (5 marks)

(b) Briefly explain why this sacred text is a document of faith. (10 marks)

B.

(a) Outline **one** religious ceremony in which the sacred text you have named above is used. (10 marks)

(b) Describe **two** ways in which this sacred text influences the way of life of a follower of this world religion. (10 marks)

C.

◆ Buddhism   ◆ Hinduism   ◆ Islam   ◆ Judaism

Briefly describe a time of growth and development in **one** of the above world religions.

(15 marks)

Section 5

(Each question is worth 70 marks.)

1. *Religions try to provide answers to the questions people ask in their search for meaning in life.*

   State one such question and outline the answer **one** of the following world religions might give to this question:

   ◆ Buddhism   ◆ Hinduism   ◆ Islam   ◆ Judaism   (2005)

2. ◆ Buddhism   ◆ Hinduism   ◆ Islam   ◆ Judaism

   Discuss the importance of a sacred text in **one** of the above major world religions that you have studied.   (2009)

3. ◆ Buddhism   ◆ Hinduism   ◆ Islam   ◆ Judaism

   Describe a time of the year that is important for members in **one** of the above world religions. In your answer you should explain why that time of year is important for followers today.   (2007)

4. You have been asked to write an article about a leader in **one** of the following world religions:

   ◆ Buddhism   ◆ Hinduism   ◆ Islam   ◆ Judaism

   In your article you should outline the role of the leader in relation to **two** of the following points:

   Community structure   Follower/discipleship   Tradition   (2003)
   (Consult Section A, Part 5, pp. 14–15).

5. ◆ Buddhism   ◆ Hinduism   ◆ Islam   ◆ Judaism

   Discuss how the style of leadership in **one** of the above world religions is influenced by the views of its founder/earliest followers.   (2006)

6. A tradition can be described as a long-established belief or custom. Describe **one** tradition that is popular in one of the following world religions that you have studied. Explain its origins and its significance for followers today.

   ◆ Buddhism   ◆ Hinduism   ◆ Islam   ◆ Judaism   (2004)

SECTION D

The Question of Faith

1 The Situation of Faith Today

- To understand the meaning of religious belief and practice.
- To know the factors that influence the religious beliefs and practices of adolescents.
- To understand the reasons for and extent of the changes in religious belief and practice in Ireland today.

- Religious belief – involves the acceptance of a set of doctrines (teachings) as set out in the sacred texts of a particular religion.
- Religious practice – how people express their religious beliefs through prayer, participation in communal worship and doing good works.

Factors influencing adolescents' religious beliefs and practices

Family

- Parents are the <u>primary</u> educators of their children, so they have an influence on every aspect of their development.
- Parents are <u>role models</u> (lead by example) for instance by taking religious beliefs seriously and regularly attending communal worship.

Peer group

Teenagers value and want each other's <u>approval</u>.

Mass <u>media</u>

What young people <u>see, hear and read influences</u> the way they view themselves and the world.

School

- Offers <u>opportunities to learn</u> about the different religions and discuss moral issues.

- Encourages participation in religious practices such as prayer, worship, pilgrimages and retreats.

Changes in religious belief and practice in Ireland

- Fewer people regularly attend daily or weekly religious rituals (e.g. Mass for Catholics).
- Fewer people display religious art (e.g. statues, paintings) in their homes.
- Fewer people practise religious teachings about fasting and abstinence (e.g. during the Christian season of Lent).
- There has been a steep decline in the number of vocations to the priesthood and religious life in the Catholic Church.
- Very few religious programmes are broadcast on national television.

However, religion still serves a function in the lives of many people:

- to mark important life events, e.g. the birth of a child, or the marriage of a couple.
- as a source of comfort in times of personal tragedy, e.g. the death of a loved one.

2 The Beginnings of Faith

aims
- To appreciate the role religion plays in the human search for meaning.
- To know about the sources of meaning in human life.

Religion and the search for Meaning

Religion has its root in the human desire to ask questions about the meaning of life and to seek answers to them.

key point

Reflection – taking time to think about the meaning and direction of our lives.

We are faced with two kinds of questions: problems and mysteries. For example:

Problem: *How can a disease be cured?*

Given sufficient time, resources and imagination, this question can be answered by scientists.

Mystery: *Why do bad things happen to good people?*

This question raises huge issues. It has proved to be beyond the ability of even the greatest thinkers to answer it satisfactorily. This is where religions come in. Each religion seeks in its own way to help us gain insights into life's mysteries so that we may grow in our understanding of them.

The sources of meaning in human life

Loving relationships: these affirm our sense of self-worth and leave us secure in the knowledge that someone is there for us in both good times and bad.

Wealth: money and property can give us a feeling of security and raise our social status.

Work: this can give us a sense of achievement. Through wage increases and promotion, work gives us a sense of security and raises our social profile.

The arts: music, drama, painting and literature can help us to express and explore ideas about who we are and what we believe. We can be awed or inspired by the experience of beauty.

Religion: devout (dedicated) members of a particular religion claim that their faith is central to their lives because it:

- inspires them to live up to their potential
- gives them the strength to face life's challenges
- offers them hope of life after death.

The Growth of Faith

- To understand the meaning of religious faith.
- To know about the stages in the development of faith from childhood through adolescence to maturity.
- To appreciate the diversity of our images of God, both personal and in the world religions.

Religious faith involves belief in God, love of God, trust in God's goodness, and acceptance of God's plan for each individual.

The stages of faith

This is a general outline of the growth and development of a person's faith.

Stage 1: Childhood faith (Birth to 12 Years)

- Young children tend to believe what they are told by adults they trust.
- The example of parents/guardians and older siblings is very important: they help children to develop their religious identity and sense of self-worth.
- At this stage children learn and come to understand the stories, beliefs and practices of their particular religion.

Stage 2: Adolescent faith (13–18 Years)

- Young people begin to wonder about life and question what they have been told. They strive to develop their own understanding of their religion and what it demands of them.
- This may lead to a strengthening of their faith or to a partial or even complete rejection of it.
- At this stage their family's commitment to living out the teachings of their particular religion is vitally important as it offers support and encouragement at a confusing time in their lives.

Stage 3: Mature faith (19+ Years)

- Most people have worked out what they believe and value and why they do so.
- They are committed and strive to live according to their religious faith.
- At this stage most people are confident about their own beliefs and are respectful of those whose beliefs differ from their own.

Personal images of God

As a person's faith matures, his/her image of God normally changes.

A child might imagine God as:

- a nice <u>old man</u> with a <u>beard</u> who sits on a throne in the <u>clouds</u>
- someone who is only interested in <u>catching people out</u> if they do something wrong
- a <u>shoulder to cry on</u> when things go wrong but someone you ignore the rest of the time.

Some people continue to see God in this way even in adulthood. However, a person of mature faith realises that God is none of these things. God is far greater than any of these inadequate images can convey. God is the greatest mystery of all.

Images of God in world religions

HINDUISM

- Hindus are free to worship different gods.
- The most prominent Hindu gods are Brahma (the Creator), Vishnu (the Preserver) and Shiva (the Destroyer).
- All the different gods and the entire universe itself are expressions of something greater – Brahman (the World Soul).
- Brahman is the impersonal source of all things and the energy that sustains all things.
- The goal of human life is to achieve nirvana, i.e. to be absorbed into Brahman after death.

BUDDHISM

- According to the Theravada tradition, the Buddha was a holy man who rejected belief in a god or gods.
- According to the Mahayana tradition, the Buddha was a god. There are elaborate systems for worshipping him.

THE MONOTHEISTIC RELIGIONS

Judaism, Christianity and Islam are all monotheistic religions. They agree that God is the loving, just and all-powerful creator and sustainer of the universe.

- Monotheism – belief in the existence of one God only.

Judaism

God's name – Yahweh – is too holy to be spoken. Instead, Jews refer to God as Adonai (the Lord).

Islam

- The Shahadah states, 'There is no God but Allah and Muhammad is his prophet.'
- Muslims believe that the Qur'an is literally the word of God.

Christianity

There are two key Christian teachings about God – the Incarnation and the Trinity.

The Incarnation

- Christians believe that in Jesus of Nazareth, God became a human being and that Jesus is God made man.
- This does not mean that Jesus is part God and part human.
- It does mean that Jesus is both fully God and fully human. He is 'true God and true man' (Catechism of the Catholic Church).

The Trinity

- The Apostles' Creed sets out the doctrine (teaching) of the Trinity.
- Christians worship only one God, but they believe that there are three distinct persons in the one God: God the Father, God the Son, and God the Holy Spirit.
- Each person reveals God relating to the world in a different way.

4 The Expressions of Faith

- To identify the different kinds of religion.
- To appreciate the different ways of expressing religious faith.
- To know the life stories of people of faith drawn from different world religions.

key point

- Polytheism – belief in the existence of two or more gods.

The expression of religious faith

People express their religious faith in any of the following ways:

- devotion to prayer
- involvement in regular communal worship
- commitment to living according to the moral teaching of their religion.

Life stories of people of faith

Mohandas K. Gandhi – Hindu tradition

- Born in India in 1869. Educated at the University of London. A lawyer by profession.
- Was involved in opposing the racist policies of the South African government for 20 years until his return to India in 1915.
- Achieved great renown as a Hindu holy man and religious teacher. Popularly referred to as the Mahatma ('the Great Soul').
- Became leader of the Indian National Congress in 1920. Led its campaign to achieve India's independence from the British Empire.
- Developed satyagraha ('steadfastness in truth'), which advocated non-violent resistance.
- Believed that refusing to retaliate violently would eventually defeat an opponent, though it would demand great sacrifice and suffering.

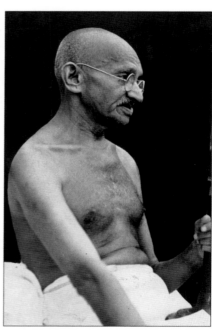

Mahatma Gandhi

- Led protest marches against unjust British policies and organised boycotts of British goods.
- Was imprisoned on many occasions by the British authorities.
- Credited as the architect of Indian independence when it was achieved in 1947.
- Assassinated by a Hindu extremist on 30 January 1948.

Mother Teresa – Christian tradition

Mother Teresa

- Born in Yugoslavia in 1910.
- Decided to become a Catholic nun.
- Trained by Mercy Sisters in Rathfarnham, Dublin.
- Became a secondary school principal in Kolkata (Calcutta).
- Referred to 10 September 1946 as her 'Day of Decision': asked permission to work with the poor in the slums of Kolkata.
- Trained to be a nurse and returned to Kolkata in 1948.
- Established a new religious order, the Missionaries of Charity, with the Pope's approval, in 1950. All sisters wear white saris edged with blue stripes. In addition to vows of poverty, chastity and obedience, they take an extra vow of pledging service to the poor.
- Opened first home for the dying in 1952. Expanded services as the order grew. Set up hospitals to care for lepers, and schools for slum children.
- Awarded Padmashri (Lord of the Lotus) by the Indian government for her work with the poor.
- Awarded Nobel Peace Prize in 1979.
- Died in 1997. Her religious order now cares for the poor in over 200 centres worldwide.

5 Challenges to Faith

Note: Chapter 5 is for Higher level students only

- To know why people believe in God's existence.
- To understand the meaning of secularism, humanism and fundamentalism.
- To know about the origins of the conflict between religion and science.
- To understand the impact of the theory of evolution on Christians' interpretation of the Creation story.

- **Theism** – belief in the existence of God.
- **Atheism** – rejection of belief in the existence of God.
- **Agnosticism** – the belief that it is impossible for us to know whether God exists or not.
- **Materialism** – the idea that only material things, i.e. things we can touch and see, are real. States that there are no spiritual realities such as God or an afterlife.
- **Secularism** – the idea that organised religion should have no direct influence on people's everyday lives or play any significant role in areas such as education and healthcare.

Reasons for belief in God

The Jewish, Christian and Muslim religions teach that God is a pure spirit. In other words, God does not have a physical body. While they admit there is no direct evidence that God exists, they claim that there is indirect evidence to support belief in God.

Consider the following:

- **The existence of the world** – the world did not simply come into existence by itself. Things only happen because something else makes them happen – the world was created by God.
- **The evidence of order and design in the world** – consider all the factors that make life possible on earth, such as the delicate balance of gases or the earth's position relative to the sun. This did not happen by accident. The world was designed and ordered in this way by God.

Humanism

Humanism refers to a set of beliefs that denies the claims made by all traditional organised religions. Generally speaking, humanists are atheists, though not all atheists are humanists.

Humanist ideas:

- The growth of secularisation is a positive development: religion has been and continues to act as a barrier to human progress.
- There is no need to believe in God or an afterlife. People can be happy and fulfilled without any religious dimension to their lives.
- Morality is a code for living that has been invented entirely by human beings. Issues of right and wrong can be decided by human reason alone, without any reference to God.

Religious people profoundly disagree with the humanist outlook. They claim that:

- Religion can be a trustworthy guide to living a good life.
- Religion has been and continues to be, a great force for good and a vital source of hope in people's lives.

Conflict between religion and science

Origins: Galileo

- Until the seventeenth century, most people accepted Aristotle's model of the universe. He said that the earth stood still at the centre of the universe and the sun and other planets rotated around it.
- Galileo Galilei (1564–1642) was an Italian astronomer. He used the newly invented telescope to study the movements of the planets.
- Galileo claimed that Aristotle's model was wrong. He said that the earth goes round the sun, not the other way round.

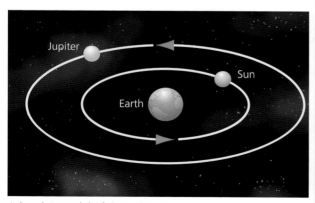

Aristotle's model of the universe

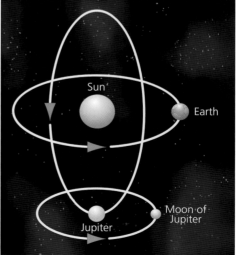

Galileo's model of the universe

HL

- Catholic Church authorities had taught for centuries that the earth was the centre of the universe. They <u>feared</u> that people's <u>confidence</u> in the Church as a source of guidance would be shattered. So they <u>ordered</u> Galileo to say that his discovery was only a hypothesis (possible explanation) and that it <u>could not be proved.</u>
- At first Galileo agreed to do this. Later, he changed his mind. In 1632, Galileo published a book in which he stated that it is a fact that the earth orbits the sun.
- The Catholic Church authorities <u>put Galileo on trial</u> for contradicting them.
- Under threat of torture, Galileo was forced to <u>recant</u> (take back what he had said). He remained under <u>house arrest</u> for the rest of his life.
- The Catholic Church later apologised for its actions and accepted Galileo's findings. However, the incident left a lasting mark on the way in which some people view the relationship between religion and science. It encouraged the view that religion and science are at best <u>rivals</u>, and at worst enemies.

Fundamentalism

- In 1656 the Anglican <u>archbishop</u> James Ussher used the dates and times given in the Bible to calculate that our world began on <u>23 October 4004 BCE.</u>
- However, <u>scientists</u> studying the fossilised remains of long-extinct creatures (e.g. dinosaurs) have concluded that the earth is far older and that it was formed about <u>4.5 billion years ago.</u>
- Some Christians, Jews and Muslims are still convinced that the Creation story in the Old Testament book of Genesis should be <u>taken literally</u> (accepted word for word). This attitude to a sacred text is called fundamentalism.

The Theory of Evolution

- Charles Darwin was one of the most influential scientists in history. He presented his ideas about evolution in two books: *On the Origin of Species* (1859); and *The Descent of Man* (1871).
- His theory of <u>evolution</u> said that all life (including humans) had evolved over millions of years by the process of natural selection (where plants, animals and people adapt to suit their environment).
- His work challenged the <u>literal reading of Genesis</u>, so many religious people rejected it at first.
- Later, scientists revised certain aspects of Darwin's work, and many religious people came to accept some form of the theory of evolution.

Charles Darwin

- In 1996, Pope John Paul II recognised that there has been so much research to support the theory of evolution that it can no longer be doubted. However, he said that while the human body is the product of evolution, each individual human soul is created by God.

The meaning of the Creation story

The Creation story in the Book of Genesis is common to Jews, Christians and Muslims. It does not offer a scientific account of the origin of life on earth. It was never intended to be read in a literal way. Rather, it offers us a poetic account designed to convey important religious teachings:

1. God created the world from nothing.
2. God's creation is good – human beings, not God, brought moral evil into the world.
3. God created human beings in his own image and likeness by giving them the powers of reason and free will.
4. God has given human beings a special place in creation with the responsibility to act as stewards of the earth (see page 132).

Two approaches to the relationship between religion and science

- Conflict: religion and science offer two opposing systems of belief. A person must accept one and reject the other.
- Partnership: religion and science need each other. Each answers different questions. For example, the theory of evolution explains *how* life began and the Creation story in Genesis explains *why* life began. Each contributes something to our understanding of life. Religion and science are partners in the search for truth.

HL Past Exam Questions

Section 1 (All questions carry 5 marks each)

1. To trust is to have confidence in something.

   True ✓   False ☐

2. A worldview can be described as a set of assumptions which a person holds about the basic make-up of the world.

   True ✓   False ☐

3. Reflection can be described as a human characteristic that involves a person thinking and becoming aware of his/her own feelings and actions.

   True ☐   False ✓

4. In religious traditions, revelation (see page 6) means __the way in which God chose to make himself known__

5. One factor which influences religious practice is __peers__

6. Brahman is associated with which one of the following world religions?

   Islam ✓   Judaism ☐   Hinduism ☐

7. Agnosticism holds the view that _____

8. Atheism holds the view that God exists.

   True ☐   False ✓

9. Religious fundamentalism holds the view that __the Bible is a factual account to be taken literally__

10. A humanist holds the view that when looking for meaning in life people should **not** turn to the supernatural or belief in God.

    True ✓   False ☐

Section 2

1. This is a photograph of a young girl playing with a balloon. (2003)

   A. Pick **one** thing from the photograph which suggests that this is an experience of awe and wonder for the girl.

      _____

      _____

      _____
      (2 marks)

   B. Some experiences that might make a person react with awe and wonder are a birth, the beauty of nature, and music. What does the expression 'awe and wonder' mean?

      _____

      _____
      (2 marks)

   C. Experiences of awe and wonder make people ask questions about the meaning of life. Give examples of **two** such questions.

      i. _____

      _____

      ii. _____

      _____
      (6 marks)

2. This is a photograph of young people holding candles.

   A. Pick **one** thing from the photograph which suggests that this is an example of inter-faith dialogue.

      _____

      _____

      _____

      _____
      (2 marks)

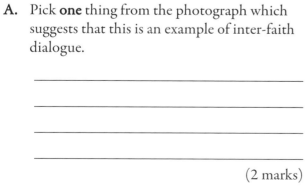

HL

B. What is reflection?

_____

_____

(2 marks)

C. Give **two** reasons why it is important for a person to have time for reflection.

i. _____

_____

ii. _____

_____

(6 marks)

Section 4

1. (2009)

A.

◆ Family   ◆ Friends   ◆ Media   ◆ School

Choose **three** of the above and explain how each can influence the religious beliefs of a teenager.   (15 marks)

B.

(a) In religious traditions the term 'monotheism' means

belief in ~~many~~ ^{one} god _____ (5 marks)

(b) Outline **one** example of how monotheism can be seen in a world religion you have studied.   (12 marks)

C.

Describe **one** way in which humanism could challenge a person's religious belief.
(18 marks)

2. (2008)

A.

Buddhism ⬭   Hinduism ⬭   Islam ⬭   Judaism ⬭

Imagine you are doing a project on the creation of the world. Tick ✔ one of the above world religions and outline **two** points it teaches about the creation of the world.   (16 marks)

B.

Outline **two** points that science teaches about the creation of the world.

(16 marks)

C.

Describe **one** similarity between what a religion says and what science says about the creation of the world. (18 marks)

3. (2006)

A.

Briefly explain how religious faith can grow out of the questions that a person asks in his/her search for meaning. (16 marks)

B.

Describe **two** other factors that can influence personal faith. (16 marks)

C.

People today express the search for meaning in many ways. Give **two** examples of how the search for meaning is expressed in today's world and give a brief account of each example. (18 marks)

Section 5

(Each question is worth 70 marks.)

1. Imagine you are preparing a talk about religious belief in Ireland today. Outline what you would say about each of the following points. (2008)
   i.   Changing patterns of religious belief in Ireland today.
   ii. Challenges to religious belief in Ireland today.

2. In a letter to a newspaper a religious leader recently wrote: '...*Young people have so much to offer, I would like to see them become more involved in the expression of religious belief...*'
   Write a response to this letter discussing the factors that might influence teenagers to become either more or less involved in the expression of religious belief. (2005)

3. Imagine you have been asked to talk, at a parent's night in a primary school, about the difference between the faith of a child and that of a teenager. Outline the talk you would give, describing **two** things that could influence the way in which a child's faith might develop into a more adult faith. (2003)

4. Examine how the religious belief of a person could be challenged by each of the following: (2009)
   i.   Agnosticism.
   ii. Atheism.

5. *'The world is charged with the grandeur of God.'* – Gerard Manley Hopkins

   Describe the key beliefs about God held by believers in **one** of the major world religions that you have studied. In your answer you should outline how the beliefs about God influence the way of life of followers of the world religion. (2007)

6. *Religion and science have points in common and points of difference in their understanding of creation.*

   Outline **one** point in common and **one** point of difference. (2006)

SECTION E

The Celebration of Faith

1 The World of Ritual

aims

- To understand the purpose of a place of worship.
- To recognise the differences between places of worship in the Christian tradition.
- To know about the key Christian festivals.
- To understand the meaning and purpose of pilgrimage.

key point

- Sacredness – the sense that a person, place or thing should be treated with the utmost care and respect.
- Place of worship – either a building or an outdoor site where the members of a particular religion express their beliefs through prayer and ritual.

Places of worship in Christianity

- Most Christians worship in a building called a church.
- The earliest Christian churches date from the fourth century CE.
- Before then, Christians had been persecuted and had to worship in secret places.

There are significant differences in the architecture and decoration of churches in the different Christian traditions.

A Catholic church

A Presbyterian church

1. Non-conformist Christians (e.g. Presbyterians) worship in simple buildings that are plainly decorated. The pulpit is the focal point of the building because non-conformist worship emphasises listening to the Word of God.

An Orthodox church

2. Catholic and Orthodox churches are more ornate, with paintings, statues, stained-glass windows and shrines. Although the pulpit is important, the altar is the focal point.

3. Orthodox churches have few seats (most worshippers are expected to stand) and a feature called an iconostasis. This is a screen, decorated with pictures, that separates the main part of the church from the sanctuary (the altar area).

Place of worship in Hinduism

- Hindus worship in a mandir (temple). However, Hindu puja (acts of worship) can also take place in the home.
- Food and flowers are offered as an expression of devotion to the gods.
- The mandir serves as both a place of worship and a community meeting place.

The key features of a mandir are:

- Primary shrine – only the priests may enter the shrine room. They awaken, bathe, dress, feed and put the statue of the god to sleep.
- Rath – a ceremonial chariot used to process the statue of the god at festival times.
- Trees – honoured because they give life and offer shelter.

A mandir

- Secondary shrine – if the temple is dedicated to Vishnu, this will be for Shiva, and vice versa.
- Nandi – figure of the bull. Revered in Hindu culture for his strength. Usually found alongside shrines to Shiva.
- Memorial shrine – dedicated to deceased local holy men. (Their bodies are usually cremated and the ashes scattered in the River Ganges.)

Key Christian festivals

The liturgical year

The liturgical year is the annual journey through religious rituals in which Christians:

- recall events in the life of Jesus Christ and the beginnings of the Christian religion
- celebrate Jesus living in his church today
- are invited to grow closer to him in worship.

Advent

Advent starts the liturgical year. It is a four-week period leading up to Christmas, during which Christians reflect on their lives and prepare to celebrate Jesus's birth.

Christmas

This celebrates the birth of Jesus. The name comes from an Old English expression meaning the 'mass of Christ'. The date of the feast itself is 25 December, but the exact time of year when Jesus was born is unknown.

It includes the feast of the Epiphany (which commemorates the Magi, or wise men, worshipping the infant Jesus).

Ordinary time

This covers 60 per cent of the liturgical year and is divided into two periods. It focuses on different aspects of Jesus's life and teachings, especially his parables and miracles.

Lent

A time of preparation for Easter. It lasts 40 days (not including Sundays), beginning on Ash Wednesday. It should involve prayer, fasting and doing charitable works.

Easter

The most important part of the liturgical year. All the other events in Jesus's life derive their significance from his having died and risen from the dead.

Easter is a moveable feast that must be celebrated on the first Sunday after the first full moon after the Spring Equinox (between 22 March and 25 April).

It includes the feasts of the Ascension and Pentecost (the birthday of Christian religion).

Pilgrimage

A pilgrimage is a journey made by a believer to a place that his/her religion considers holy. A pilgrim is a person who goes on a pilgrimage, either alone or as a member of a group.

Places of pilgrimage

A place may become a centre of pilgrimage for different reasons, for example:

- it is associated with an event in the life of a holy person or the founder of a particular religion
- it is the burial place of such a person.

Usually pilgrims go to pray at a shrine – a religious monument that commemorates an important event or holy person associated with that place. For example:

- the Kaaba in Makkah for Muslims
- the Via Dolorosa in Jerusalem for Christians.

Reasons for pilgrimage

People go on pilgrimage for a variety of reasons:

- to seek God's forgiveness for past sins
- to ask for God's guidance
- to gain strength from God
- to revitalise their faith.

Christian places of pilgrimage

The Holy Land is the most frequently visited pilgrimage site for Christians who want to retrace the footsteps of Jesus. The main sites are:

- Bethlehem – Church of the Nativity
- Nazareth – Basilica of the Annunciation
- Jerusalem – Via Dolorosa (Way of Sorrows) and Church of the Holy Sepulchre.

Another important centre is Rome, where the headquarters of the Catholic Church is located in the Vatican. Important sites here include: the Basilica of St Peter; the Sistine Chapel; the Catacombs.

Pilgrimage sites in Ireland

Important pilgrimage sites in Ireland include: Croagh Patrick; Lough Derg; Downpatrick; Knock.

Marian shrine

Croagh Patrick, Co. Mayo:

- Croagh Patrick has been a popular pilgrimage site since the Middle Ages.
- It is said to have been a place where St Patrick came to pray.
- Pilgrims are expected to walk barefoot along a steep four-kilometre track to the mountain top (some 765m above the surrounding countryside).

Knock, Co. Mayo:

- Knock is a Marian shrine – a holy place dedicated to Mary, the mother of Jesus.
- It is said to have been the site of an apparition (appearance) of Mary on the evening of 21 August 1879. No message was given but some people claim to have been cured after visiting the site.
- Pope John Paul II celebrated Mass there in 1979.

2 The Experience of Worship

- To understand the meaning of worship and ritual.
- To be able to provide examples of ritual in the world's religions.
- To understand what it means to participate in a ritual.

- **Worship** – involves any action by which people: engage in a relationship with God; show that they recognise the importance of God as creator and sustainer of the universe; respond to God through prayer and ritual.
- **Ritual** – a formal religious ceremony, approved by religious authorities, which gives a regular pattern to people's worship of God.

Examples of religious ritual

- Hinduism – bathing in the River Ganges.
- Judaism – touching the mezuzah before entering a home.
- Buddhism – removing one's shoes before entering the shrine room of a temple.
- Christianity – blessing oneself when passing a church or graveyard.
- Islam – performing wudu (ritual washing) before praying in a mosque.

The sacraments as public rituals

The word sacrament means 'a holy mystery'. Catholic and Orthodox Christians believe that there are seven sacraments.

In these sacraments Christians recall and re-enact the life, death and resurrection of Jesus Christ. The sacraments also celebrate the presence of Jesus in the key moments of people's lives:

1. Baptism – birth.
2. Confirmation – growth to maturity.
3. Eucharist – living and sharing with others.
4. Reconciliation – failure and forgiveness.
5. Matrimony – marriage and family.
6. Holy orders – sacred ministry.
7. Anointing – illness, healing and death.

Participation in worship

Participation means taking an active role in ritual. For example, in the Catholic Church one may be involved as:

- a bishop or priest officiating at a ritual such as the Mass.
- a lay person (non-ordained member) acting as a minister of the Word (reading from a sacred text), minister of the eucharist (distributing Holy Communion), altar server or member of the choir.

3 Worship as a Response to Mystery

Note: Part 3 is for Higher Level students only

- To appreciate how participation in worship is a response to our experience of mystery in life.
- To understand the meaning of revelation.
- To know one story of an encounter by a human being with the mystery of God.

- Wonder – a feeling of awe we experience when we encounter something extraordinary or profound.
- Mystery – a question or experience that raises matters so deep and profound that it surpasses our human capacity to comprehend and answer fully.

Worship as a response to mystery

Experience

We can encounter the mysterious invisible presence of God in our lives through encounters with the beauty of the natural world, the power of the elements and the goodness of fellow human beings. God reaches out to each of us through the natural world and the many people we encounter.

Catholics and Orthodox Christians believe they encounter the presence of God in a special way through the eucharist.

The Catholic Church teaches that at the consecration during the Mass, through the power of the Holy Spirit and the action of the bishop/priest:

- the <u>bread</u> ceases to be bread and becomes the <u>body</u> of Jesus
- the <u>wine</u> ceases to be wine and becomes the <u>blood</u> of Jesus.

This is the doctrine of transubstantiation. When Catholics receive the eucharist at Holy Communion in the form of bread and wine, they believe they are receiving the body and blood of the risen Jesus himself, who is as really present to them as he was to the disciples two thousand years ago.

Response

We can communicate with God through prayer and active participation in public rituals. These include the celebration of the eucharist (for Catholics, Orthodox and Anglicans), attending prayers at a mosque (for Muslims) or at a synagogue (for Jews), or praying privately at home.

We often do not need to voice our gratitude in words. Sometimes an experience is so powerful that our only response is an awed silence and quiet meditation on what we have encountered or witnessed.

We can respond in gratitude to God for the beauty of his creation by doing all in our power to preserve it, e.g. reducing environmental pollution and protecting endangered species.

The meaning of revelation

Revelation is the way God reaches out to human beings and reveals things about his nature that human beings could otherwise never know.

Revelation is necessary because God is so totally different from anything else in human experience. (For example, human beings live in time while God does not; God is eternal.) As a result, if we were left to our own devices, human beings would know very little about God.

God has revealed his presence to human beings through:

- prayer and meditation
- sacred texts
- miracles.

Encounter with the mystery of God

Example: God calls Moses (Judaism)

- God called Moses to begin his mission to free the Jewish people from captivity in Egypt and to lead them to the Promised Land (Exodus 3).
- God appeared to Moses in a strange and mysterious way as 'a blazing bush' which 'was not burnt up'.
- In this account, God (Yahweh) is revealed to be both awe-inspiring and loving.

4 > Sign and Symbol

aims

- To understand the meaning of sign and symbol.
- To identify and explain the symbols of the major world religions.
- To understand the symbolism of icons.
- To appreciate the richness of symbolism in the sacraments.

key point

- Sign – a concrete image, word or gesture that points beyond itself but has only **one** fixed, clear and unambiguous meaning, e.g. a red light at a road junction means 'stop'.
- Symbol – a concrete image, word or gesture that points beyond itself but has **more than one** meaning and so is richer in content than a sign, e.g. a national flag such as the Irish tricolour.

The symbols of the major world religions

Religion	Symbol	Explanation
Judaism	Menorah	A seven-branched candlestick that stood in the Temple in Jerusalem in ancient times. The central branch represents the Shabbat, the day on which God rested after creating the world.
Christianity	Cross	Jesus died on the cross, a shameful and painful death. Christians believe that by dying in this way, Jesus redeemed humankind and demonstrated his power over sin, suffering and death.
Islam	Crescent moon	Muslims say that Islam guides a person's life just as the moon and stars guide a traveller at night in the desert. This symbol on a country's flag often indicates that it is a Muslim state.

Religion	Symbol	Explanation
Hinduism	Aum 	The written form of the sacred sound 'Aum'. According to Hindu texts, Aum was the first sound, out of which the rest of the universe was created.
Buddhism	Eight-Spoked Wheel	The Buddha spoke of an Eightfold Path to enlightenment. This is traditionally represented as an eight-spoked wheel. The path is a guide to living life compassionately and non-violently.

The symbols of Christianity

Cross/Crucifix

- The cross is almost always found in Christian places of worship.
- Jesus died on the cross. Through his death and resurrection God showed his power over sin, suffering and death.
- A crucifix is a cross with a figure of Jesus hanging from it.

The fish

- This was perhaps the most popular symbol among early Christians.
- The Greek word for fish is *ichthys*.
- Each letter of the word points to a name or title for Jesus.

Greek Letter	English Letter	Greek Word	English Translation
I	I	Iesos	Jesus
X	Ch	Christos	Christ
Θ	Th	Theou	Of God
Y	Y	Yios	Son
Σ	S	Soter	Saviour

This means: **Jesus Christ, God's Son, Saviour.**

Ashes on Ash Wednesday

- Ash Wednesday is the first day of Lent.
- Catholics attend Mass and their foreheads are marked with ashes.
- This is done to remind them that, though following Jesus involves suffering, the way of the cross leads to new life, to resurrection and eternal life with God.

The meaning of icons

- The word icon comes from the Greek word meaning 'image'.
- An icon is a richly decorated painting of Jesus, Mary, a saint, an angel, or a combination of these religious figures.
- Every detail in an icon is intended to convey an important religious idea. Consider the Teaching Christ (16th century, Moscow school) in the picture.
- The doctrine of the incarnation teaches that Jesus is true God and true man. Gold and blue colours are used to suggest that Jesus is divine.
- The humanity of Jesus is suggested by the brown, earthy colour that is used for the inner garment.
- Icons are widely used by Christians in the Orthodox tradition to help them focus their minds on the mystery of God.

Encountering symbols in the sacraments
Baptism

- The word baptism comes from the Greek word *baptizo*, which means 'to dip'.
- Baptism may be received only once. It is a ritual of naming, welcoming and thanksgiving.

In each stage of the ritual, symbols serve a specific purpose.

1. The parents present the child for baptism and are welcomed by the priest.
2. Also present are the godparents, who promise to help in bringing up the child as a Christian.
3. The child is anointed twice, with oil of catechumens (symbolising the strength that comes from God's grace); and oil of chrism (symbolising the call to live by God's standards).

4. The parents and godparents renew their own baptismal vows and commit themselves to educate the child in the Christian faith.

5. Water is poured over the child's head to symbolise the purifying power of the Holy Spirit. Then the child is formally named.

6. A white shawl is wrapped around the child as a symbol that he/she shares in the resurrection of Jesus.

7. A candle is lit to remind all present that Jesus's resurrection is a guarantee that death is not the end but a gateway to eternal life with God.

8. The priest blesses the child to remind those present that the child belongs to, and is a gift from, God.

Confirmation

- Confirmation comes from the Latin word *confirmare*, meaning 'to strengthen'.
- Confirmation is a sacrament of initiation and may be received only once.
- Since the Middle Ages, the Catholic Church has offered the sacrament of confirmation to young Catholics entering their teenage years.
- The Orthodox Church continues the earlier practice of baptising and confirming in the same ceremony.

The ceremony in the Catholic Church consists of the following elements. Each symbol has a specific purpose.

1. Renewal of baptismal vows: the young person is thought to be ready to make these on his/her own.

2. The stretching out of hands: the bishop asks for God's grace to strengthen a person to fulfil his/her vocation (calling).

3. Anointing with chrism: this symbolises the power of the Holy Spirit strengthening the young person in his/her commitment to follow Christ.

5 Prayer

- To understand the reasons why people pray.
- To know the six types of prayer.
- To describe the experience of prayer in different religions.
- To appreciate the importance of prayer in the life of an individual.

key point

- Prayer – communication from the heart between human beings and God. Two elements: giving thanks and praise to God; and seeking help and forgiveness from God. It can be either formal or informal.
- Personal prayer – praying alone to God.
- Communal prayer – praying to God in the company of others.
- Meditation – silent prayer where one calms one's body to achieve inner quiet before reflecting on some experience or sacred text.
- Contemplation – the highest form of meditation, involving no words at all, just a sense of being in union with God.

Reasons for prayer

People usually pray for one or more of these reasons.

- Shock caused by an experience of suffering.
- Sorrow for some wrong they have inflicted on others.
- Gratitude when something important works out.
- Joy at having the love of another person.
- An experience of the awesome beauty and power of nature.
- Realisation of how short and swiftly ended life can be.

The six types of prayer

1. Adoration: a sense of mystery and wonder.
2. Intercession: love for other people and a wish to help them.
3. Petition: awareness of our own needs.
4. Contrition: a realisation of where we have gone wrong in our lives and a desire to do better in future.
5. Protection: a sense of the power of evil and an awareness of the suffering it causes, and of our need for the strength that only God can give.
6. Thanksgiving: a deep gratitude to God for all those people and things that are important to us.

Prayer in different religions

Judaism

Devout Jews pray three times each day, following the example set for them by the patriarchs:

- in the morning, because Abraham prayed early in the morning
- in the afternoon, because Isaac stopped his work to pray in the afternoon
- in the evening, because Jacob thanked God in the evening.

They do this to demonstrate and strengthen their commitment to keeping the covenant that God made with their ancestors.

Islam

According to the Qur'an, a Muslim must pray five times each day – at dawn, noon, mid-afternoon, sunset and evening.

In Muslim countries, the muezzin calls the faithful to prayer. Attendance at Friday prayers is compulsory. Men and women worship separately. On arrival at the mosque, Muslims remove their shoes, put on skullcaps and perform wudu (ritual washing) to prepare their minds and bodies. Kneeling on mats, they face in the direction of Makkah.

After the imam's sermon, they recite prayers according to a set format, each gesture saying something about a Muslim's relationship with Allah. For example:

- standing: to show alertness to the words of Allah
- bowing: to demonstrate love and respect for Allah
- prostration: to show surrender to Allah
- sitting: to indicate tranquillity and acceptance of the will of Allah.

The importance of prayer in the life of an individual

Through prayer, people can build and sustain a strong relationship with God.

Ignatius of Loyola (1491–1552)

Background

Ignatius, a Spanish nobleman, was born in the castle of Loyola near the Pyrenees in Spain. Orphaned at an early age, he was raised by foster parents. As a young man he led a carefree lifestyle and showed very little, if any, interest in prayer.

Significant moments

- Ignatius became a professional soldier. In 1521 he suffered a severe leg wound in battle and was brought home to Loyola to recuperate.
- During his long convalescence, Ignatius read the gospel accounts and biographies of saints. This changed his outlook on life. He decided to dedicate the rest of his life to serving God.
- Ignatius spent a year at the monastery of Manresa, where he prayed for God's guidance. While there he also wrote the first draft of his book, *The Spiritual Exercises*.
- Ignatius then went to Paris where he studied to become a priest.
- He later gained permission from the Pope to establish a new religious order called the Society of Jesus (the Jesuits).
- The order grew rapidly. Jesuits set up schools and universities and spread Christianity throughout South America, India, China and Japan.

St Ignatius of Loyola

The spiritual exercises

- All Jesuit students since Ignatius's time have gone through the steps outlined in this book.
- They are a series of meditations on key passages of the New Testament.
- In the course of a month-long retreat, people are asked to use their imagination to place themselves into the events described in each scriptural passage.

The structure of the exercises is:

- Week 1 – sin and forgiveness.
- Week 2 – Christ's kingship.
- Week 3 – Christ's passion and death.
- Week 4 – Christ's resurrection.

Past Exam Questions

Section 1 (All questions carry 5 marks each)

1. In religious traditions, the term 'sacred' means _____

_____

_____

2. To worship is to show a lack of religious belief.

   True   False ☑

3. Read the list of places of pilgrimage and the list of world religions given below. One place of pilgrimage has been matched to the religion with which it is most associated as an example for you. Make **one** other match.

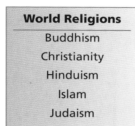

Places of Pilgrimage
Bethlehem
Bodh Gaya
Mecca
River Ganges
Western Wall

World Religions
Buddhism
Christianity
Hinduism
Islam
Judaism

Example:

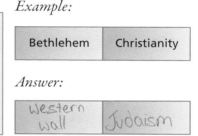

Bethlehem	Christianity

Answer:

Western Wall	Judaism

4. Read the list of religious festivals and world religions given below. One festival has been matched to the religion with which it is associated as an example for you. Make **one** other match.

Religious Festivals
Easter
Passover
Eid ul-Fitr
Diwali
Wesak

World Religions
Buddhism
Christianity
Hinduism
Islam
Judaism

Example:

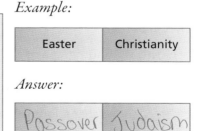

Easter	Christianity

Answer:

Passover	Judaism

5. Read the lists of religious symbols and world religions given below. One religious symbol has been matched to the religion with which it is associated as an example for you. Make **one** other match.

Religious Symbols
Cross
Star of David
Crescent moon
Eight-spoked wheel
The Aum

World Religions
Buddhism
Christianity
Hinduism
Islam
Judaism

Example:

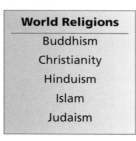

Cross	Christianity

Answer:

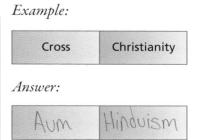

Aum	Hinduism

HL

6. In religious traditions, an 'icon' is _a religious painting_

_____

7. Baptism is an example of a Christian sacrament. Name another Christian sacrament. _reconciliation_

8. In religious traditions, 'contemplation' is a type of prayer which involves

_____

_____

_____

9. A prayer of penitence is a prayer which expresses sorrow for wrongdoing.

True [✓]   False [ ]

10. Read the list of prayers and the list of world religions given below. One prayer has been matched to the world religion with which it is most associated as an example for you. Make **one** other match.

Prayers
The Our Father/ The Lord's Prayer
The Shahadah
The Shema
The Paritta
The Rig Veda

World Religions
Buddhism
Christianity
Hinduism
Islam
Judaism

Example:

The Paritta	Buddhism

Answer:

Our Father	Christianity

Section 2

1. This is a photograph of the monastery in Clonmacnoise, Co. Offaly.

   A. State **one** thing from this photograph which shows that Clonmacnoise is a place of religious importance.

   _____

   _____

   _____

   (2 marks)

   B. Name **one** other place of religious importance.

   Lough Derg

   (2 marks)

C. Give **two** reasons why the place you have named above has religious importance for people.   HL

i. _____

_____

ii. _____

_____

(6 marks)

2. This is a photograph of clothes that are worn during religious ceremonies.

A. Pick **one** thing from this photograph which suggests that these clothes are designed to be worn during religious ceremonies.

_____

_____

(2 marks)

B. Name **one** religious ritual that takes place during a religious ceremony.

_____

_____

(2 marks)

C. Give **two** reasons why people use religious rituals to express their faith.

i. _____

_____

ii. _____

_____

(6 marks)

3. This is a photograph of a young person taking part in a Sacred Thread ceremony.

A. Pick **one** thing from the photograph which shows that this ceremony is celebrating religious faith.

_____

_____

(3 marks)

HL

    B. Name **one** other ceremony which celebrates a stage in the growth of religious faith.

_____

(3 marks)

    C. Taking part in a religious ceremony is one way of expressing religious faith. Name **two** other ways of expressing religious faith.

       i. _____

        _____

      ii. _____

        _____

(4 marks)

Section 3

(This section is worth 50 marks.)

Read the following extract from a letter and answer *all* the questions below.

'. . . I'm just back from the Christmas Carol Service. Even though it was cold, just about everyone was there. When we all stood to sing "O Come All Ye Faithful" I thought of you; I know it's your favourite Christmas carol.

'The children from the local school decorated a Christmas tree with special symbols. Each symbol stood for a person from the Bible who was looking forward to the coming of the Messiah. All the parents looked very proud watching their children place stars, harps, etc. on the branches of the tree. Two teenagers read a commentary about each of the people represented on this special tree, which is called a Jesse tree.

'Rev. Farrell read modern poems and prayers, as well as readings from the Bible. The whole community was represented in the procession to put the figures into the crib. The figures of Mary and Joseph were carried by a newly married couple who have just moved here. I thought it was nice to include them in that way. Members of a local band even wrote their own carol for the occasion. You could see that it meant a lot to everyone.

'We lit candles for friends and family members who weren't with us. I lit a candle for you, all those miles away. I didn't need to say anything. Just lighting the candle, and watching its flame, was enough for me to know that you would have a good Christmas too.

'When I shook hands with people as a sign of peace, lots of people asked me to give you their best wishes and to wish you a happy Christmas. During the sign of peace the local youth group brought up boxes of toys and food which they had collected for people in need.

'I hope you liked the present I sent you. I also included a tiny bit of straw from the crib. I'm sure you were wondering what it was. I thought it would remind you of all those you know, who love you and who are thinking about you as they celebrate Christmas . . .'

1. What evidence is there in this letter to suggest that Christmas is a time of religious importance? (12 marks)

2. (a) What evidence is there in this letter to show that the carol service was an example of communal prayer? (10 marks)

   (b) Give **one** example of a symbol that was used during the carol service and explain what it means. (10 marks)

3. Give **two** reasons why people worship.

   i. _____

   _____

   ii. _____

   _____
   (6 marks)

4. How does this letter show what is meant by **one** of the following:

   ◆Religious belief   ◆Wonder   (12 marks)

Section 4

1. (2009)

A.

Buddhism ⬭ Christianity ⬭ Hinduism ⬭ Islam ⬭ Judaism ⬭

   (a) Tick ✔ **one** of the world religions above that you have studied.
   Name **one** symbol associated with the world religion you have ticked above.

   _____ (5 marks)

   (b) Describe the meaning of the symbol you have named above for members of the world religion with which it is associated. (15 marks)

   (c) Explain **two** reasons why people use a symbol to express religious faith. (16 marks)

B.

Communal prayer ⬭   Personal prayer ⬭

Tick ✔ **one** of the above and outline what is involved in this type of prayer. (14 marks)

HL 2. (2008)

A.

(a) Tick ✔ **one** of the following major world religions you have studied and name a time of year that has religious importance for its members.

Buddhism ⬭   Christianity ⬭   Hinduism ⬭   Islam ⬭   Judaism ⬭

Name of time of year _____   (5 marks)

(b) Describe **one** way in which members of a major world religion mark a time of year that has religious importance for them.   (15 marks)

(c) Outline the religious meaning of **one** ritual that marks an important time of year for members of a major world religion.   (15 marks)

B.

People have different ways of participating in worship – gestures, music, readings, etc.

Explain how **one** way of participating in worship can help people to communicate with God.   (15 marks)

3. (2007)

A.

(a) Give **one** example of a symbol people use when they are praying.   (5 marks)

(b) Explain why people use the symbol you have given above when they are praying.   (9 marks)

B.

Suggest **two** reasons why people can sometimes find it difficult to pray.   (12 marks)

C.

(a) Meditation ⬭   Penitence ⬭

Tick ✔ **one** of the above types of prayer that you have studied.

Outline what is involved in the type of prayer you have ticked above.   (10 marks)

(b) Outline **two** reasons why prayer is important for members of a world religion that you have studied.   (14 marks)

4. (2006)

A.

'When I worry I pray . . . I feel guilty praying because I'm always asking for something . . .'

'Silence plays a big role for me in prayer, because if you listen hard enough you will hear God speak back to you.'

Source: Veritas

Why is prayer important in the life of a person who has religious belief? (15 marks)

B.

Buddhism ⬜ Christianity ⬜ Hinduism ⬜ Islam ⬜ Judaism ⬜

Tick ✔ **one** world religion you have studied from those listed above and name the place of worship where members of this world religion regularly gather for prayer.

(a) Name of place of worship _____ (5 marks)

(b) Describe the place of worship you have named above. (15 marks)

C.

Explain how the place of worship you have described above can help people to pray. (15 marks)

Section 5

(Each question is worth 70 marks.)

1. *I feel at home in a Hindu temple. I am aware of Presence, not personal . . . but something larger. – Yann Martel*

   Outline how places of worship help people to respond to the experience of mystery in life. (2005)

2. *Ritual can help people to express their faith.*

   Discuss the importance of ritual for members of **one** of the following major world religions: (2007)

   ◆Buddhism   ◆Christianity   ◆Hinduism   ◆Islam   ◆Judaism

3. *Communal prayer and worship show what a community believes and values.*

   Discuss this statement referring to **one** community of faith you have studied. (2006)

HL

4. *In worship people sometimes give expression to their experience of mystery in life.*
   i.   Examine how **one** situation in life could be an experience of mystery for a person.
   ii. Describe **one** example of worship and explain how it allows a person to express the experience of mystery in life. (2009)

5.

    ◆Prayer of Petition   ◆Prayer of Praise   ◆Prayer of Thanksgiving

Examine how **two** of the above types of prayer express the religious beliefs of a major world religion you have studied. (2008)

6. Examine the importance of prayer for members of **one** of the following world religions you have studied.

◆Christianity   ◆Buddhism   ◆Hinduism   ◆Islam   ◆Judaism

Your answer should describe **two** different types of prayer that are important in this tradition and explain why they are important for its members. (2003)

7. Name an important person in the spiritual tradition of **one** of the following world religions and describe how he/she contributed to the understanding of prayer in his/her religious tradition. (2004)

◆Buddhism   ◆Christianity   ◆Hinduism   ◆Islam   ◆Judaism

SECTION F

The Moral Challenge

1 Introduction to Morality

- To understand the meaning of morality.
- To appreciate the distinction between a moral and a non-moral action.
- To understand the role of values.
- To know the factors that influence our values.

key point

- Human relationships – the way we are connected to, or involved in, each other's lives. Our relationships can be (a) interpersonal (between individual people); (b) communal (among a group of people); (c) global (extending worldwide and involving different countries).
- Morality – a set of beliefs or standards that offer us guidance on whether an action is the right or wrong thing to do.
- Freedom – our capacity to choose whether to do one thing or another.
- Influence – any factor that affects the choices we make.

Moral and non-moral actions

Morality is concerned only with moral actions, not with non-moral ones. People can be held <u>responsible</u> for the consequences of their moral actions, i.e. praised/rewarded if they are right/good and blamed/punished if they are wrong/bad.

Non-moral actions

Example: accidentally slipping and falling off a ladder.

This is a non-moral action because the person does not make a free and deliberate choice and is <u>not in control</u> of what he/she is doing.

Moral actions

Example: rescuing someone from a burning building.

In this example the person does make a <u>free and deliberate choice</u>; he/she is <u>in control</u> of the action. Therefore the action is moral: in this case morally right, since it results in saving another person's life.

The role of values

A person's moral actions are profoundly influenced by the values that they hold. Their values may lead them to perform certain actions or not perform other actions.

A value is anything considered to be good, desirable, important or worthwhile. For example:

- a doctor who values her patients' lives and health will do her utmost to care for them
- a businessman who values dedicated and skilled workers will offer them the pay and conditions needed to retain them in his company.

Important influences on our values

Socialisation refers to the process by which people acquire their values and learn how to behave towards others. Significant influences on our values include:

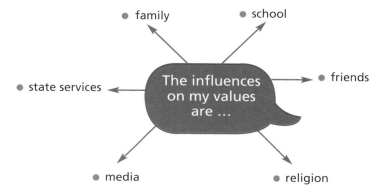

2 Sources of Morality

Sources of our moral vision

Family

This is the first place where people learn how to interact with others. They normally learn to treat others with compassion and respect.

Friends

Genuine friendships can build up people's self-confidence and self-worth. They can help people to be more considerate towards others and give them the encouragement needed to do right rather than wrong.

School

Going to school provides people with an opportunity to develop their minds, learn to co-operate with others and acquire the knowledge and skills needed to make the right choices when faced with difficult decisions.

Religion

This offers answers to life's great questions and can shape a person's whole outlook on life. It provides a moral vision to help guide people's behaviour with a view towards making the world a better place for all.

Media

The media (i.e. television, the internet, etc.) can powerfully affect people's priorities. They can encourage a self-centred approach to life, but they can also help people to be better informed about important issues and encourage them to be active participants rather than passive spectators.

State

In its laws, the state sets limits on people's behaviour by permitting certain activities and prohibiting others. However, people need to distinguish between what is legal and what is morally right. They are not always the same.

Examples of moral vision

The Golden Rule

- Whether their moral vision is religious or non-religious, almost all people accept the Golden Rule as the fundamental principle of any system of morality.
- Traditionally the Golden Rule has been stated as: 'Do unto others as you would have them do unto you.'
- The basic idea of the Golden Rule is that people should have respect for, and show compassion towards, one another.
- All religions have some version of this rule. However, there are differences between them as to how it should be applied to particular moral issues such as abortion, capital punishment and war.

The moral vision of Judaism

The Torah contains hundreds of rules for living. These are summarised in the Ten Commandments:

1. I, the Lord, am your God; you shall have no other gods besides me.
2. You shall not take the name of the Lord your God in vain.
3. Remember to keep holy the Sabbath day.
4. Honour your father and your mother.
5. You shall not commit murder.
6. You shall not commit adultery.
7. You shall not steal.
8. You shall not bear false witness against your neighbour.
9. You shall not covet your neighbour's wife.
10. You shall not covet anything that belongs to your neighbour.

The Commandments can be divided into two groups:

1. The first three set out what is meant by genuine love of God.
2. The other seven deal with how people should love and respect one another.

Example of a source of moral guidance

The Magisterium in the Catholic Church

The Magisterium is the official teaching authority of the Catholic Church. It consists of the Pope and the college of bishops under his leadership.

Catholics distinguish between the Extraordinary Magisterium and the Ordinary Magisterium.

Extraordinary Magisterium

- Catholics believe that when the Pope speaks ex cathedra (using his full authority as successor to the apostle Peter) on matters of faith and morals, he is protected from error by the Holy Spirit.
- In this situation his statements are believed to be infallible (free from error) and must be accepted by all Catholics.

Ordinary Magisterium

- This concerns non-infallible statements issued by the Pope offering guidance to Catholics on moral issues.
- Since Catholics believe that God speaks to them through the teachings of their Church, they are expected to treat these statements with respect, carefully study and accept them.
- A papal encyclical is the name given to a special letter written by the Pope that offers Catholics guidance about religious and moral issues.

Formal and informal codes

- An informal code is a self-imposed, unwritten set of rules that we assume in our interactions with others, e.g. good manners.
- A formal code is one imposed on us by society in a set of written rules which state how we should behave, e.g. safety regulations in the workplace; rules of the road.

key point

A code is a set of guidelines setting out how we should behave.

Development of formal codes

One of the earliest known formal codes is the Code of Hammurabi, which can be traced back to 1700 BCE. It set out the rights and duties of all people within a kingdom that once covered much of the Middle East. It also offered protection to the weak and poor from abuse by the powerful and wealthy. Many crimes were punishable by death under it.

One important recent code is the Universal Declaration of Human Rights.

- *Universal* – it applies to all people <u>everywhere</u> in the world, whatever their race, creed, sex or social status.
- *Human rights* – the things we <u>need</u> to live a fully human life.

The declaration was signed by the representatives of all nations on earth. Its sets out 30 basic rights to which all people are entitled. These include freedom of assembly and freedom of thought and expression.

aims

- To understand the meaning of moral growth.
- To identify the stages of moral growth.
- To understand the meaning of moral maturity.
- To be able to distinguish between the different kinds of conscience.

key point

- Moral growth – the process by which we acquire the knowledge of what is right and wrong and develop the ability to distinguish between them.

How moral growth occurs

Moral growth is a gradual process. From an early age we experience many influences on our moral development. We learn right from wrong by:

- following the example set by people we trust, e.g. family and friends
- learning from the consequences of our own actions and those of others
- accepting the rules laid down by our parents, school, religion and society.

The stages of moral growth

Stage 1: Infant

As infants, we are entirely self-centred. We are only aware of, and seek satisfaction of, our immediate needs or wants, e.g. food, warmth and companionship.

Stage 2: Child

As children, we gradually begin to develop some understanding of right and wrong. We gain a greater awareness of how our actions have consequences for both ourselves and others. However, the expectation of reward or punishment largely determines our moral choices.

Stage 3: Young adult/teenager

As young adults, we should grow in self-confidence and self-worth. We should be able to distinguish right from wrong in more complex moral situations, and appreciate the consequences of our actions. However, the approval of our peer group remains a significant influence on our moral choices.

Moral maturity

As a person grows older, he/she should become <u>less</u> preoccupied with <u>material</u> values (e.g. money and property) and develop a <u>greater</u> appreciation for <u>spiritual</u> values (e.g. love and compassion). However, people do not automatically become more morally mature as they grow older.

A morally immature person is motivated by:

- a <u>selfish</u> desire to satisfy his/her needs to the exclusion of those of others,
- a <u>fear of punishment</u> or <u>desire for reward,</u>
- a <u>longing to gain</u> the <u>approval</u> of others.

In contrast, a morally mature person:

- is <u>committed</u> to doing what is <u>right</u>
- <u>respects both</u> him/herself and others
- takes into account <u>rules</u> made to promote good and prevent evil
- is willing to <u>evaluate honestly</u> the situation in the light of his/her own convictions
- <u>considers the consequences</u> before acting.

Conscience

Types of conscience

Conscience – the ability to apply our values to a particular moral problem and make a decision about the right thing to do.

1. *Properly informed:* we have achieved moral maturity. We seek to inform ourselves as fully as possible before making any decision. The moral decision we make must be consistent with our values.

2. *Lax:* we have consistently acted selfishly and have become desensitised to the whole issue of whether something is right or wrong.

3. *Legalistic:* our decision-making processes are dominated by a rigid, closed-minded, rule-keeping approach to life. While it can give us a great sense of security, it can also make us blind to following the right course of action.

4 ▷ Religious Morality in Action

- To understand the process of making a moral decision.
- To appreciate the difficulties faced when making a moral decision.
- To understand how a moral vision can influence decision-making in two situations.
- To know about the work done to achieve peace and reconciliation.

- Decision-making – the process we go through to figure out what we should do in a given situation.
- Truth – that which is the case, whether or not anyone wants to acknowledge it.
- Justice – treating people fairly by respecting their rights.
- Sin – any freely chosen, deliberately intended and selfish action whose consequences we desire, which inflicts harm on ourselves and/or others and weakens/destroys our relationship with God.
- Forgiveness – to cease to feel anger and no longer desire retribution against others and pardon them for having harmed or offended us.

Making a moral decision

Stage 1 *Situation* – What exactly is the problem facing me?

↓

Stage 2 *Information* – Do I have all the relevant facts?

↓

Stage 3 *Guidance* – Where can I get reliable advice? What does the law say? What does my religion teach?

↓

Stage 4 *Aim* – What do I want to achieve? What is my goal?

↓

Stage 5 *Motive* – Why am I doing this? Is it just or unjust?

↓

Stage 6 *Method* – What is the right way to achieve this?

↓

Stage 7 *Impact* – How will my actions affect other people?

Difficulties in making moral decisions

Certain things can cloud our judgment and make it difficult to know what is the right choice to make. There are four main areas of difficulty:

1. *Knowledge* – Do we understand the true nature of the problem we face?
2. *Emotions* – Do we allow our feelings to have too great an influence on our decisions?
3. *Peer pressure* – Do we only make a particular choice in order to conform with others or win their approval?
4. *Reasoning* – Are we aware of how easy it is to make a mistake when trying to decide the right thing to do?

The influence of moral vision on two decisions

Example 1: Stewardship of the environment

The environment is the world and everything in it. The principal environmental problem facing us now is climate change.

The approach of Jews, Christians and Muslims to solving this problem is profoundly influenced by the religious moral vision they all share. The Tenakh, the Bible and the Qur'an all remind their readers that:

- the environment is a gift to us from God who created it,
- the environment is sacred, i.e. worthy of total respect,
- human beings are not the owners of the environment: we are God's stewards, i.e. we have a special responsibility to care for the world on God's behalf.

Only by taking all this to heart can we develop a new relationship with the earth that will ensure that it is passed on in a healthy and fertile state to future generations. Practical steps to achieve this include:

- conserving non-renewable resources
- initiating afforestation programmes (planting trees on non-forest land)
- recycling where possible
- using biodegradable products
- joining environmental protection groups
- voting for political candidates who are genuinely committed to protecting the environment.

Example 2: War

War means 'armed hostilities between two groups in which each side puts people forward to fight and kill'. The consequences of war include:

- loss of human life
- physical and mental suffering of the survivors
- a refugee crisis (people fleeing their country for safety)

- destruction of property
- enormous debt.

Just war theory

One influential Christian response to the question of whether or not we should engage in warfare is called the just war theory. This aims to:

'The Peaceable Kingdom' by Edward Hicks

- identify conditions under which it is morally right to go to war
- put limits on how people wage war so as to minimise the harm inflicted.

According to the just war theory, a Christian may only engage in warfare if the following conditions can be fulfilled:

1. *Just cause:* The reason for which the war is fought should be good and worthwhile.
2. *Right intention:* The aim of those going to war must be to restore peace and achieve justice. It must not be an act of revenge.
3. *Last resort:* All peaceful alternatives to war must have been tried and failed.
4. *Likelihood of success:* There must be a reasonable hope that the war can be won.
5. *Principle of proportion:* The war should be fought by fair means and inflict the minimum of suffering.
6. *Safety of non-combatants:* Civilians should never be intended targets.

Working for peace and reconciliation

Peace is 'the absence of violence and the provision of space and resources to allow human life to flourish'. One place dedicated to the pursuit of peace is the Glencree Centre for Peace and Reconciliation in Co. Wicklow.

Glencree is a non-profit, non-governmental organisation which was founded in 1974 in response to the sectarian (inter-religious) violence that afflicted Northern Irish society.

Glencree is devoted to peace-building and reconciliation, not only in Ireland but also in the wider world. It does so by facilitating dialogue and offering groups the space to help deal with their conflicts. Although it began by fostering links between Catholics, Anglicans and Protestants, it now welcomes all religious traditions.

Glencree has also created peace education programmes. Its motto is: 'If we waged peace with the intensity with which we wage war, then there would be no wars.'

5 Law and Morality

Note: Part 5 is for Higher Level students only

- To explain the part played by the civil law and the Constitution.
- To understand the meaning of libertarianism and religious fundamentalism.
- To describe the relationship between religious morality and the law.

- Civil law – a rule set out by the state authorities, permitting some forms of behaviour and prohibiting others, which all its citizens are obliged to obey. A legal action is one that is in accordance with the civil law.
- Constitution – a document that sets out all the basic rights of citizens and sets limits to the power of the state in order to safeguard its citizens' rights.
- Libertarianism – the view that we should be free to think and behave as we choose without undue interference from the state, as long as we do not interfere with the equal rights of other citizens.
- Religious fundamentalism – the view that the ideal form of society is a theocracy (where the moral code of the majority religion in a state is embodied in its civil law).
- Pluralism – the view that no one group should be allowed to dominate a society and that all different groups should have equal influence. The aim is for the civil law to encourage the different groups (races, religions, etc.) to live together in peace.

Religious morality and the law

All the major world religions teach that their members should strive to be good citizens of whatever state they live in. However, they also caution them to remember that:

- the state does not have the final say on what is right and wrong
- there is a higher standard for distinguishing right from wrong, which has been set by God.

Therefore, people should not blindly obey the laws of the state. They should ask whether a law is morally acceptable, i.e. whether it is fair, just and works for the benefit of all citizens.

There are many instances in history of governments using the law of the state to deprive citizens of their rights unjustly.

HL We are obliged to obey the law of the state when it insists on behaviour that upholds the common good. When the law of the state fails to do so, it is morally justifiable to refuse to obey a particular law. Sometimes it is necessary to disobey a particular law in order to highlight an injustice and replace it with a better, more just law.

Opposition to an unjust law

- The black community in the United States, led by Dr Martin Luther King, Jr (1929–68), conducted a campaign of non-violent protest to resist unjust laws that deprived them of important civil rights.

Martin Luther King leading a demonstration against discrimination

- This began with a boycott of the bus system in Montgomery, Alabama in 1956. This happened because local police arrested a black woman, Mrs Rosa Parks, when she refused to obey a law that required her to give up her bus seat if a white person wanted it.
- The black community refused to be treated as second-class citizens in their own country.
- Dr King believed in the Christian moral vision. This states that everyone is created equal in the eyes of God. He demanded equal rights for all people – black and white.
- He organised and led massive rallies, marches, sit-ins and petitions to put pressure on the US government to reform the country's laws.
- In 1957, the US Supreme Court ordered an end to laws discriminating against black passengers on public transport.
- In 1964, the Civil Rights Act granted equal rights to all American citizens.
- In recognition of his role in this, Dr King was awarded the Nobel Peace Prize.

Past Exam Questions

HL

Section 1 (All questions carry 5 marks each)

1. Morality is a person's understanding of right and wrong.

   True [✓]   False [ ]

2. Religion can be described as a source of morality in a person's life. Name another source of morality.

   School

3. The Ten Commandments is an example of a moral code. Name another moral code.

   Ten Pillars

4. A person uses his/her conscience to _help decide what is right and wrong in a situation_

5. When a person acts with integrity, he/she behaves in a way that is dishonest.

   True [ ]   False [✓]

6. In religious traditions, to have 'authority' means _power to make important decisions_

7. A constitution of a state is a set of _set of laws_

8. The Law of Karma is a law of the state.

   True [ ]   False [✓]

9. Pluralism holds the view that _More than one religious group can co-exist_

10. A libertarian holds the view that _freedom of speech_

Section 2

1. Question 3. This drawing shows a moral code.

   A. Explain why this is an example of a moral code.

   _____

   _____

   _____

   (4 marks)

1. I am the Lord your God: You shall have no other gods before me.
2. You shall not make wrongful use of the name of the Lord your God.
3. Remember the Sabbath day and keep it holy.
4. Honour your father and your mother.
5. You shall not murder.
6. You shall not commit adultery.
7. You shall not steal.
8. You shall not bear false witness against your neighbour.
9. You shall not covet your neighbour's house
10. You shall not covet your neighbour's wife
Ex. 20:3, 7, 8, 12, 13–17.

HL

   B. Name **one** religious moral code. _____

_____

(2 marks)

   C. Give **two** reasons why a moral code is important in a community of faith.

     i. _____

_____

    ii. _____

_____

(4 marks)

2. This is a photograph of a religious sister comforting a death-row prisoner.

   A. State **one** thing from the photograph which suggests that the sister is comforting the prisoner.

   _____

   _____

(2 marks)

   B. Give **two** reasons why a religious person would work with prisoners in this way.

     i. _____

_____

    ii. _____

_____

(4 marks)

   C. Suggest **one** positive effect this work could have on the prisoner.

_____

(4 marks)

3. This photograph shows an example of stewardship.

   A. Pick **one** thing from the photograph which shows that this is an example of stewardship.

   _____

   _____

   _____

(2 marks)

B. What is stewardship?

_____

_____

(4 marks)

C. Give **two** other examples of stewardship.

i. _____

_____

ii. _____

_____

(4 marks)

Section 4

1. (2009)

A.

(a) Religion can influence a person's view of what is right and wrong in a situation. Name **one** other influence on a person's view of what is right and wrong.

(5 marks)

(b) Buddhism ☐   Christianity ☐   Hinduism ☐

Islam ☐   Judaism ☐

Tick ✔ **one** of the world religions above that you have studied.

Describe **one** example of the work for *either* justice *or* peace being done by members of the world religion you have ticked above.   (10 marks)

(c) Explain **two** reasons why members of a world religion would work for *either* justice *or* peace.

i. _____

_____

ii. _____

_____

(10 marks)

B.

(a) In religious traditions the term 'stewardship' means

_____caring for God's planet_____

(5 marks)

(b) Outline **one** example of stewardship in a community of faith that you have studied. (10 marks)

C.

Explain **two** reasons why stewardship is important for a community of faith.

i. _____

_____

ii. _____

_____
(10 marks)

2. (2008)

A.

Outline what the term 'conscience' means. (10 marks)

B.

(a) Explain how a person's religious faith could influence his/her conscience. (12 marks)

(b) Apart from religious faith, explain how **one** other factor could influence a person's conscience. (12 marks)

C.

Describe **one** way in which a person's conscience can develop as he/she grows older. (16 marks)

3. (2007)

A.

Outline what is involved in **two** stages of the process a person goes through in making a moral decision. (18 marks)

B.

(a) Give **one** example of a situation where there could be conflict between a country's law and a religion. (12 marks)

(b) Pluralism ⬭   Religious Fundamentalism ⬭

Tick ✔ **one** of the above and outline how it sees the relationship between a country's law and a religion. (20 marks)

4. (2006)

A.

Moral codes express the rights people are entitled to, as well as the responsibilities they have towards others.

(a) Name **one** moral code you have studied.

_____

(5 marks)

(b) State **one** right it expresses.

_____

(5 marks)

(c) State **one** responsibility it expresses.

_____

(5 marks)

(d) Explain how the moral code you have named above could help a person in making a moral decision. (10 marks)

B.

(a) Outline a situation in which a person has to make a moral decision.

(10 marks)

(b) Explain how a person's religion could influence his/her moral decision-making in the situation you have outlined above. (15 marks)

Section 5

(Each question is worth 70 marks.)

1. Analyse the ways in which a religious moral code expresses the beliefs of a world religion you have studied. (2009)

2. Show how a community of faith can help its members to respond to a situation in which truth **or** peace may be threatened in today's world. (2005)

3. Outline the work being done by **one** community of faith to promote justice. In your answer you should describe the religious moral vision on which this work is based. (2007)

4. Discuss how *either* the search for truth *or* the search for peace has been a driving force in the life of a person of faith in a world religion you have studied. (2006)

5. (a) Outline what libertarianism sees as the relationship between personal morality and a country's law.

   (b) Examine how there might be conflict between the libertarian point of view and a country's law on **one** moral issue you have studied. (2008)

6. Outline the work for peace of **one** religious leader or community of faith. In your answer you should describe the religious moral vision on which this work is based. (2003)

Sample Exam Paper: Questions and Answers

Section 1

There are three types of question in this section: tick the correct box; fill in the answer; and make a match (all 5 marks each)

Tick the Correct Box

1. A world view can be described as a set of assumptions which a person holds about the basic make-up of the world.

   True ✔   False ☐

2. Historical evidence for the existence of Jesus of Nazareth can be found in the writings of:

   Hosea ☐   Isaiah ☐   Tacitus ✔

3. The Last Supper was a meal associated with which of the following religious celebrations?

   Bar Mitzvah ☐   Hanukkah ☐   Passover ✔   Sukkot ☐

4. The river Ganges is sacred to which of the following world religions?

   Christianity ☐   Hinduism ✔   Islam ☐   Judaism ☐

5. The Law of Karma is a state law.

   True ☐   False ✔

6. Morally mature people think only of themselves in making decisions.

   True ☐   False ✔

Fill in the answer

1. In religious traditions martyrdom means *dying/giving one's life for one's religious beliefs.*

2. In religious traditions a division or major split between people of the same faith is known as a *schism.*

3. Materialism means *following a way of life that seeks fulfilment or happiness through acquiring wealth, i.e. money and property.*

4. The Dalai Lama is associated with which world religion? *Buddhism.*

5. Libertarianism is *the view that we should all be free to do as we choose, without undue interference from the state, so long as we do not interfere with the equal freedom of others.*

Make a match

1. Read the list of religious objects and world religions given below. Match any **one** object to the religion with which it is associated.

Religious Objects	Religions
Arti lamp	Buddhism
Baptismal font	Islam
Mezuzah	Hinduism
Prayer mat	Christianity
Stupa	Judaism

Answer:

Any **one** of these:

Arti lamp	Hinduism
Baptismal font	Christianity
Mezuzah	Judaism
Prayer mat	Islam
Stupa	Buddhism

2. Read the list of religious celebrations and the list of world religions given below. Match one celebration to the religion with which it is associated.

Religious Celebrations	Religions
Diwali	Buddhism
Easter	Christianity
Eid ul-fitr	Hinduism
Rosh Hashanah	Islam
Wesak	Judaism

Answer:

Any **one** of these:

Diwali	Hinduism
Eid ul-fitr	Islam
Easter	Christianity
Rosh Hashanah	Judaism
Wesak	Buddhism

Section 2

A. Study the picture given and answer the questions accompanying it.

This is a photograph of Muslim pilgrims at the Grand Mosque in Makkah (Mecca).

A. Pick **one** thing from the photograph which shows that this is a holy place.
(2 marks)

Your answer should include any **one** of the following:

- It shows the Kaaba in Makkah.
- It is an Islamic shrine covered in a black cloth.
- There are many pilgrims gathered around it.
- The pilgrims are wearing a special seamless white garment called the ihram.

B. State **two** reasons why people go on pilgrimage.

Give any two of the following (2 marks per reason):

- To fulfil the fifth Pillar of Islam, which is to go on the Hajj at least once in one's lifetime.
- To seek God's help in facing some life crisis.
- To grow closer to God through prayer and doing penance.
- It is a tradition in many religions to go on pilgrimage.

C. Identify **two** rituals associated with pilgrimage.

Give any two of the following (2 marks per ritual):

For a Muslim when on pilgrimage to Makkah:

- Bathing on arrival at Makkah to show one's intention to complete the pilgrimage.
- Putting on the ihram and walking barefoot.
- Passing around the Kaaba seven times.
- Passing between the hills of Safa and Marwa seven times.
- Throwing stones at the pillar in the village of Mina.

For a Catholic on pilgrimage in Knock, Co. Mayo:

- Attending Mass.
- Reciting the Rosary.
- Attending the Sacrament of Reconciliation.
- Fasting overnight.

Section 3

Read the extract given and answer all the questions below it.

'We were coming to the end of our three-day workshop on how to build and sustain community. The young people who had attended were preparing to say their goodbyes. Aminu quietly approached us and asked if we would give him a moment to speak to those present before they left. We had just spent three days focusing on the importance of respect for each other, so it didn't take long for a hush to descend on the hall.

'"I found it difficult to come here," he began. "As a Muslim it is not easy to come to a centre that is run by Christians. We had been warned that Christians would attack us or try to convert us. I only came here because a good friend assured me I would be safe and no one would try to change my faith."

'I felt myself growing anxious. Had someone offended Aminu's beliefs? Was he angry and hurt? The main goal of our three days together was to encourage the participants to understand, appreciate and respect each other's different ways to God. Had it somehow gone wrong? Instead of understanding and healing, had the end result left this young Muslim feeling hurt and betrayed? I was greatly relieved when I heard his next words.

'"In these days," Aminu said, "I have found out that I do not have to be afraid of Christians. I know this because something truly wonderful happened to me yesterday. Yesterday, as you know, was Friday – our holy day. I had been wondering how I would make my way to the mosque when one of the Catholic priests came and offered to drive me to my afternoon prayer. I could not believe my ears. And that is what he did. He took me in his car to the mosque. I know that there are people in my village who will never believe that such a thing happened. It is something I will never forget and I wish that this good work we have been doing these past three days will reach many more young people. May Allah bless you all."

'I looked around the room. Everyone was nodding their heads in approval and smiling. Then I remembered these words from the New Testament: "Faith without actions is dead," said St James; "Have a profound respect for one another," said St Paul; "Love one another as I have loved you," said Jesus. Sometimes it's just as simple as giving someone a lift.'

Source: Adapted from Africa magazine and Dublin Examining Board, Pre-Junior Certificate Examination, 2008

1. Identify two things that the three-day workshop hoped to achieve.

   From your reading of the text you should give the following two-part answer (5 marks per part):

   - Paragraph 1 – To help people of different faiths to learn how to build and sustain community.
   - Paragraph 2 – To encourage the participants to understand, appreciate and respect each other's different religious beliefs.

2. (a) Identify two ways in which the workshop was an example of inter-faith dialogue.

   From your reading of the text you should give the following two-part answer (5 marks per part):

   - Paragraph 1 – When a person of one particular religion (Aminu – a Muslim) began to speak, a hush descended on the hall so that he could be heard by those of other religions.
   - Paragraphs 2 and 4 – Although this workshop was held at a Christian-run centre, Muslims felt welcome and respected.

   (b) State one way in which this workshop was successful for Aminu.

   From your reading of paragraph four in the text you should offer any one of the following (worth 10 marks):

   - Aminu has lost his fear of Christians.
   - Aminu no longer fears that Christians will attack him or try to convert him.
   - Aminu realises that people of different religions can be good friends and neighbours to one another, thanks to the priest driving him to Friday prayers.
   - Aminu has gained so much from the workshop that he hopes that other young people of different religions will have an opportunity to benefit from it too.

3. Read this statement: 'Faith without actions is dead.'

   Explain (using an example) what is meant by this statement.

   In your answer (worth 10 marks) you could offer either of the following general explanations:

- To really believe in something means living by it – practising what you preach by doing good works.
- To have faith means committing yourself to living by its moral code in your daily life – as in giving a good example to others.

Another example offered in this extract:

- The priest who willingly drove Aminu to the mosque to ensure that he did not miss Friday prayers.

4. Explain how this extract demonstrates the meaning of one of the following key concepts:

◆ Communication   ◆ Reconciliation

This question is worth 10 marks: 5 marks for each point of information.

For example:

Communication:

- The workshops involve listening to one another and taking part in open-minded discussion.
- Through this the participants grow in understanding one another and learn to respect one another's different points of view.

Reconciliation:

- Before this workshop, some Muslims who attended it were distrustful of Christians and feared them.
- This workshop brought together people of different faiths, helped them to put aside their fears and prejudices and come to respect one another.

Section 4

There are six questions in this section, one for each of the six sections of the syllabus.

- Higher level – answer any *four* questions.
- Ordinary level – answer any *five* questions.

*Note: Be sure to answer **every part of each question**.*

Sample Question

The Question of Faith

A. 'When I was young everyone I knew believed in God and churches all over Ireland were crowded every Sunday . . .' (Pat, born 1940)

(a) Is there a difference between religious practice in Ireland today and religious practice when Pat was young? (Tick **one** box)

Yes ✔   No ☐

(b) Explain why you think there is/is not a difference in religious practice in Ireland today.

This question is worth 10 marks: 5 marks for each point of information given in the answer.

*Your answer should include any **two** of the following:*

- Among Catholics, there has been a sharp decline in attendance at religious services such as Sunday Mass.
- Fewer Catholic families recite the rosary together.
- Many Christians are more questioning of doctrines such as hell or the eucharist.
- Religious leaders are no longer held in the same high esteem they once enjoyed.
- Fewer homes display religious pictures and statues.
- There has been a great reduction in the number of vocations to the priesthood and religious life in the Catholic Church.
- Fewer Catholics observe the tradition of fasting and abstinence during Lent.

(c) Explain why you think that these changes have occurred.

This question is worth 10 marks: 5 marks for each point of information given.

*Your answer should include any **two** of the following:*

- The growth of **religious indifference**, i.e. some people have no interest in the issues raised by religion.
- Some people have embraced **materialism**, i.e. they see the accumulation of wealth as more important than spiritual fulfilment.
- Some people are deeply **disillusioned** by the leadership and structures of organised religion.
- Some people have embraced **individualism**, i.e. they are unwilling to put the good of society as a whole before their own desires and goals.

(d) The findings of surveys show that many young people today believe in God. Give two reasons why many young people today believe in God.

This question is worth 10 marks: 5 marks for each point of information given.

*Your answer should include any **two** of the following:*

- The universe could not simply have started by itself. Its existence can only be accounted for by saying that it was created by God.
- All the delicate balances and complex designs we can see in the natural world could only exist if they were put there by God.
- Human beings are the only creatures which have an awareness of right and wrong and the freedom to choose between them. This was given to us by God.

B. 'Outline the story of one person you have studied who dedicated his/her life to expressing their religious faith.

This question is worth 20 marks. You should provide at least 5 points of information (4 marks per point).

Examples include:

- *Mother Teresa of Calcutta*
- *Mahatma Gandhi*
- *Martin Luther King*
- *Maximilian Kolbé*
- *Catherine McCauley*
- *The Dalai Lama*
- *Brother Roger of Taizé.*

Example: Maximilian Kolbé

*Your answer should include at least **five** of the following points:*

- Born in Poland in 1894. Baptised a Catholic.
- Entered Franciscan order and studied in Rome.
- Obtained doctorates in both philosophy and theology.
- Ordained as a priest in 1918.
- Great communicator of Christian message – set up a radio station and published a daily newspaper.
- Arrested and imprisoned by Nazis in 1941.
- Prisoner number 16670 in Auschwitz concentration camp.
- Took the place of a condemned family man in the camp's death cell in July 1941.
- Led fellow prisoners in prayer and hymn-singing.
- Cared for needs of those also sentenced to death by starvation.
- Murdered with lethal injection after two weeks.
- Canonised (made a saint) in 1982.

Section 5 – Higher level only

There are six questions in this section, one for each section of the syllabus. Answer any **one** of the six.

*Note: be sure to **give the number of the question you are answering** in your booklet.*

Each question is worth 70 marks.

In your answer you should give at least **seven** points of information (10 marks per point).

HL Sample Question

Pick one of the following issues and outline the work done on this issue by a member or members of a religious organisation you have studied. In your answer you should describe the religious moral vision on which this work is based.

◆ Forgiveness ◆ Freedom ◆ Stewardship

Example:

Freedom – The work of William Wilberforce (1759–1833), Anglican social reformer.

- Religious moral vision – the outlook on life a person has based on his/her religious faith that influences what he/she believes is right and wrong.
- After education at Cambridge University, Wilberforce became an MP at the Westminster parliament in 1780.
- Four years later he underwent a great spiritual crisis and emerged a devout Anglican.
- His actions were based on the Christian moral vision which holds that human life is sacred and that each person has a dignity that should be nurtured and respected. He believed that all people are created equal in dignity by God and that slavery was a great evil.
- Wilberforce led the campaign to abolish slavery in the British empire.
- Thanks in large part to his tireless efforts, the slave trade was abolished in 1807.
- Wilberforce then turned his energies to improving the conditions of those held in Britain's jails.
- Although his life was frequently threatened by powerful enemies, Wilberforce continued his work because he believed that it was his vocation, i.e. he had been called to do it by God.